BRITAIN IN OLD PHOTOGRAPHS

CORNWALL

TOM BO

SUTTON PUBLISHING LIMITED

Sutton Publishing Limited
Phoenix Mill · Thrupp · Stroud
Gloucestershire · GL5 2BU

First published 1999

Title page: On the beach at Bude, *c.* 1908.

British Library Cataloguing in Publication Data
A catalogue record for this book is available from the
British Library.

ISBN 0-7509-2300-8

Typeset in 10.5/13.5 Photina.
Typesetting and origination by
Sutton Publishing Limited.
Printed in Great Britain by
Ebenezer Baylis, Worcester.

To my grandsons James and Adam

The Promenade, Penzance, *c.* 1920.

CONTENTS

Map of Cornwall   4

Introduction   5

1. Caradon   7

2. North Cornwall   31

3. Restormel   57

4. Carrick   81

5. Kerrier   105

6. Penwith   133

Acknowledgements   158

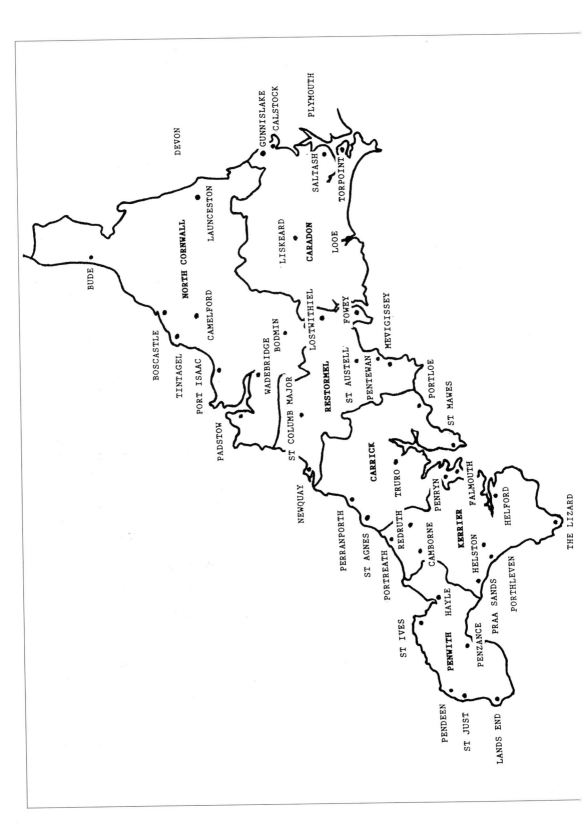

INTRODUCTION

I am still doing old photograph books! If you remember, my first two books in this series were *The Cornish Coast* and *Around Plymouth*. In this new book I have widened my scope to include the whole of Cornwall, and have selected the photographs, written the captions, and even done the acknowledgements and map; now I must introduce the book as a whole.

This publication contains 253 old photographs ranging in date from the 1880s to the 1990s. They include locations all over Cornwall and cover many subjects: harbours, shipwrecks, mines, cars, trains, personalities, etc. My prime interest is the old photograph, and what it shows. This leads me on to relate a great deal of history and local knowledge. In fact, there are many interesting stories in this book, and some surprises. I am a Cornishman writing about places and people in Cornwall and you will find me biased towards everything Cornish. I expect you will also detect many emotions. That's the way I wanted it to be, and I would like you to make your own judgement.

The timescale from the 1880s to the 1990s has given me an opportunity to look back from the millennium at over one hundred years of Cornish history. All this means in practical terms is that I have visited most of these places just before publication of this book to see how they look today. My captions therefore include comments on recent changes. There are also four of my own photographs illustrating changes over the years. My overall opinion is that Cornwall remains a beautiful place, despite increased population, more houses and heavy road traffic. The decline of small businesses, as shown by empty shops in towns generally, is one of the most obvious trends. This book has also provided an opportunity to look back at how our forefathers lived. Some died in the mines and many more were unemployed – a problem that is still with us.

The photographers who produced these images of the early twentieth century were interesting people, especially if they were Cornish or worked in Cornwall throughout their career. Therefore in this publication I have told the life stories (or as much as possible) of five prominent Cornish photographers: E.C. Argall of Truro (p. 75), E.A. Bragg of Illogan and Falmouth (p. 97), G.W.F. Ellis of Bodmin (p. 39), S.J. Govier of Chacewater (p. 117) and A.H. Hawke of Helston (p. 144). They all produced picture postcards and were successful, but their origins and lives were very different.

Cornwall is divided into six administrative districts. Each chapter of the book covers one district, from east to west, in the following order: Caradon, North Cornwall, Restormel, Carrick, Kerrier and Penwith. The Kerrier chapter is slightly longer than the others. Within each chapter the locations are also generally from east to west, and where a district has both north and south coasts I have tried to separate them with inland locations. There are some exceptions, for various practical reasons, but the map provided on page 4 should help to resolve any problems.

I have enjoyed looking at all these pictures, reading works of reference and writing my captions. I hope that all those who love Cornwall will also appreciate these old photographs and the many stories that they contain.

Southgate Street and Arch, Launceston, 1944.

Tower House, Cremyll Point, Mount Edgcumbe, *c.* 1908. The tower was demolished by a bomb during the Blitz Plymouth in 1941.

CHAPTER ONE

CARADON

The Torpoint Steamboat Company's SS Marguerite *passing Buttspill above Calstock on the River Tamar, during her maiden trip to Weir Head on 1 August 1898.*

Fore Street, Gunnislake, 1906. This pretty picture shows the town when its busy mining and quarrying industries had declined. Across the River Tamar were the famous Devon Great Consoles and Bedford United copper mines. On the Cornish side were the Gunnislake Glitters, Hawkmoor and Old Gunnislake copper mines, Drakewells tin mine, Greenhill chemical works, and Pearson's quarry. There was work for the local residents and little road traffic. Today the mines have gone and this is the main A390 road across the Tamar with four road junctions at this point and heavy traffic. Now crash-barriers dominate the scene, with good reason, and many local shops lie empty.

New Bridge, Gunnislake, 1920. The Abbot of Tavistock in 1520 decreed that this bridge be built to shorten the journey from Tavistock to Callington and Liskeard. It is very impressive with its six arches, each 23 ft above the river. There were skirmishes here between the Cavaliers and the Roundheads during the Civil War, and Charles I crossed the bridge in 1644 after winning the Battle of Lostwithiel. Today it carries the A390 from Tavistock on its way through Gunnislake up over Hingston Down to Callington. As you would expect, it is now too narrow for present-day traffic conditions.

S *Alexandra* at Weir Head, Gunnislake, *c*. 1906. This is some of the finest scenery in the West Country. Gunnislake is in the distance and we are looking down at Wier Head from the magnificent 300 ft Morwell Rocks on the Devon side of the River Tamar. Weir Head is the highest point of navigation on the river, and here the fresh water from up river changes to salt water as it flows down to Plymouth Sound. Many steamer trips from Plymouth went up to Weir Head before turning around, and the smaller craft could turn without difficulty, using their engines. Here we see SS *Alexandra*, one of the Saltash, Three Towns and District Company's large 126 ft paddle-steamers, in the process of turning. The crew needed to warp the vessel around with ropes and poles, using the small inlet created by the canal lock gates on the left side, and often crowds would gather to watch the manoeuvres. The unfortunately named Tamar Manure Navigation Company built this canal to bypass the weir and allow vessels to reach places further up river, like Gunnislake, to deliver manure (sand) and coal and load bricks from the brickworks at Bealswood nearby. It was also the intention to continue the canal northwards to join up with the Bude Canal and thereby provide a waterway right across the Cornish peninsula. However, trading requirements change, the canal fell into disuse and the company went into liquidation in 1942. The story of the Bude Canal is told in chapter two.

Morwellham Quay on the River Tamar, 1902. Benedictine monks from Tavistock Abbey founded Morwellham Quay probably as early as the eleventh century, and they used it to bring in supplies and to export their woollen cloth. The name is derived from 'Morwell' (the district) and 'Ham', which means land by the water. The monks' trade grew until Henry VIII dissolved the monasteries in the 1530s, when the king passed the Tavistock Abbey estates to the Russell family, who later became the Dukes of Bedford. There are very rich mineral deposits in this area: tin was discovered in the twelfth century, and pack-horses carried blocks of tin to Morwellham Quay for shipment. Silver and lead deposits were also found. In the early 1800s rich lodes of copper ore were found at Devon Great Consols, Bedford United and many other mines in the Tavistock area, mainly owned by the Duke of Bedford. Soon many thousands of people were working in the mines. The engineer John Taylor, who managed Wheal Friendship and other mines around Tavistock and Mary Tavy, decided to cut his cartage costs by building a canal from Tavistock through a tunnel in Morwell Down to terminate at a point 237 ft above Morwellham. There the ore was to be transferred to wagons that ran on rails down a 1:6 incline with a double track to reach Morwellham Quay. This work was carried out between 1803 and 1817 and comprised 4 miles of canal including over 1½ miles of tunnel. Fully laden ore boats went to Morwellham and returned to Tavistock with coal, lime and general goods. Similarly, the Devon Great Consols and Bedford United Mines found the carting of ore to Morwellham too slow, laborious and expensive. A 4½ mile long railway track was built to link these mines to a terminus above Morwellham and the work was completed in 1859. The drop of about 300 ft to the river level was achieved using a 1:3 incline. The mines reached the height of their prosperity between 1848 and 1858, and Morwellham was full of heaps of yellow copper ore on its way to the South Wales smelters. Also there were increasing amounts of arsenic to be used in dyes, paints and insecticides. In the 1870s and 1880s the mines started to decline as the copper lodes became exhausted, and Morwellham began to suffer through lack of business. In the 1890s only the arsenic trade kept the port going. Devon Great Consols closed in 1901 and Morwellham became deserted, as you see it in this photograph. The break in the trees at the top of the picture marks the railway terminus and the start of the railway incline. The house halfway up the hill is at the end of the canal, and shows the start of this incline. On the left is the Great Dock where 300-ton ships moored to load up from the piles of ore around the quay. The row of cottages was built by the Duke of Bedford in 1856 to house the influx of people brought to Morwellham by the copper boom. Morwellham Quay and the George and Charlotte Mine have now been restored by the Tamar Valley Trust and are open to visitors.

Calstock Viaduct, *c.* 1918. Calstock, on the Cornish side of the river, is about 2 miles downstream from Morwellham. This view is from Calstock Quay and looks downstream to Calstock Viaduct, the Danescombe Valley and Cotehele Woods beyond. The viaduct carries the Gunnislake–Plymouth railway line and was completed in 1907. It is built of concrete blocks and took 3½ years to complete. On the right is a wagon hoist which was used to transfer goods between the quay and the railway line. A railway incline had already been constructed at Danescombe in 1860 connecting the quay with the East Cornwall Mineral Railway to carry goods in and out of Calstock Quay. The ¼ mile long quay had been busy with the export of minerals such as tin, copper, arsenic, silver, lead and tungsten, as well as locally produced items including bricks, rope, granite, fertiliser, grain and market garden fruit and vegetables. The barges brought in sand, coal, limestone, timber and general goods. All this changed when the mines closed in about 1900.

A view from Calstock Viaduct in 1909, soon after its completion. This new vantage point provides a grand view of Calstock and the paddle-steamer *Prince Edward* as she makes her way downstream with her beautiful curving wake trailing away in the distance. The small quay at Calstock was for pleasure-boats and many large vessels called regularly at the quay. Sometimes on Saturdays there would be hundreds of pleasure-trippers thronging the little streets, spending their money and having a good time. Today the boats still come from the Barbican or Phoenix Wharf up the lovely River Tamar for passengers to enjoy a cream tea in the Riverside Restaurant, or a drink in the ancient Boot Inn, or maybe a walk around historic Calstock with its echoes of long ago.

Ashburton Hotel, 1919. A walk downstream along the quay at Calstock brings you to this hotel, which stands by the river at the bottom of the Danescombe Valley. It was built in 1859 to provide accommodation for trippers arriving by steamer, and has now been appropriately renamed the Danescombe Hotel. This is a reference to an ancient episode of Cornish history. The Romans left Britain in AD 410 and when the Saxons came the Cornish fought them for many years. Eventually the Cornishmen joined forces with the Danes for one last mighty effort to drive off the Saxons. In AD 838 the Danes sailed up the Tamar in their longboats, landed at Danescombe and marched up the hill to join the Cornish army. Egbert and his Saxons quickly crossed the Tamar and defeated the unlikely alliance at the Battle of Hingston Down. The Danes fled to their ships, and the Cornishmen never fought the Saxons again.

Cotehele House, 1907. This was the home of the Edgcumbe family. William Edgcumbe from Tavistock married Hileria de Cotehele, the heiress to the Cotehele estates, in 1353. Their grandson, Sir Richard Edgcumbe, was a Cornish hero and perhaps the most famous member of the family. He fought for Henry Tudor and the Lancastrians during the Wars of the Roses, and benefited from being on the winning side. His son Piers married Joan Durnford, the rich heiress to the Stonehouse estates, and the family moved to Mount Edgcumbe House in 1553.

The Royal Albert Bridge, Saltash, 1910. It was completed by Isambard Kingdom Brunel in May 1859 and is one of his best achievements on the railways. He had originally designed it as a two-track rail crossing but owing to financial restrictions he had to reduce it to a single track. Now this is the only single track line in Cornwall. Brunel made just one journey across the bridge before he died in September 1859. Below the bridge is Saltash Pier and in the distance is the training ship *Mount Edgcumbe*, which was moored off Saltash and used for training homeless and destitute boys for the navy.

Saltash Infants' School, 1935. Back row, left to right: Bill Rowe, Jack Baskerville, Harold Hoskins, Frank Appleton, Norman Fletcher, Patrick Tucker, Warwick Jones, Vernon Seccombe. Middle row: Patrick Voise, Francis Bryant, Norman Beer, Desmond Nancollas, Eddie Smale, Edwin Hart, Bill Meager, Sidney Bracegirdle, Bernard Cook, Dennis Veale. Front row: Dereck Smale, May McCarthy, Betty Sellers, Isobel Carter, Joan Francombe, Joyce Stanton, Beryl Evans, Doreen Donnelly, Arthur Bennett.

Sir John Carew Pole of Antony House, Torpoint, August 1944. When I last saw this portrait it was hanging at the top of the staircase in Antony House. It depicts Sir John in his uniform and duffle coat during the Normandy landings, where he won the DSO when commanding the 2nd Devons at Les Forges on the road to Conde. He was then Colonel Sir John Carew Pole, 12th Battalion, and was aged forty-two. After the war he commanded the 4/5th TA Battalion of the DCLI and became their honorary colonel. He held many public appointments including Chairman of Cornwall County Council, High Sheriff, Vice-Lieutenant and Lord Lieutenant of Cornwall. For nearly seventy years he was squire of the Antony Estate, and he developed the gardens and restored the house to its Queen Anne beauty and proportions by removing the unsightly Victorian wing. In 1961 Antony House was vested in the National Trust with the family remaining in residence with an agreed lease. Sir John Carew Pole died in January 1993 aged ninety. He was a charming man who was loved by all who knew him.

Restless racing in the Hamoaze, *c.* 1946. This is my father in his boat in a Torpoint Mosquito Sailing Club race. It was just after the war and Dad and others did a great deal of work to rebuild the clubhouse and get the club going again. Sometimes I was foresheet-man in the two-man crew but not often. Dad originally had a 14 ft International dinghy, a lovely little mahogany boat that needed washing out with fresh water but was light and easy to handle. He was a joiner by trade and he built a number of 17 ft boats, Flying Fifteens and high-speed motor boats. I remember one social evening in the clubhouse when the visiting guest Uffa Fox sang 'Three old ladies locked in the lavatory, nobody knew they were there'. He was more a boat designer than a singer.

Me and Mum on Torpoint Beach, 1932. We lived opposite the Ballast Pond and this scruffy old beach but I loved it, growing up with seaweed smells and up to my armpits in mud! Things lived on the beach in those days: winkles, cockles, shrimps, conger eels, crabs, seaweed and funny looking red blood-suckers! Turn over a stone and watch out: wriggly things everywhere! Now it looks more like the Somme.

Antony Road, Torpoint, 1914. This is the main A374 road going out of Torpoint, looking up the hill towards Antony. When I was a boy the houses along the main road were named Hillsborough Terrace, my school was in Albion Road on the right, and Morris's sweet shop was on the left. That reminds me of liquorice sherbets, gobstoppers, aniseed balls and acid drops. This photograph shows a slightly older Torpoint than I remember and I expect you wonder why there is a raised step in front of some houses. I think there must have been some rich car owners in Torpoint in 1914.

...my Cadets from East Cornwall at camp near St Austell, 1945. This is a group of cadets from Saltash and ...point with a number of lads from Devonport. I was aged fifteen and this is the group photograph taken when ...were at camp somewhere near St Austell. Sadly after more than fifty years I cannot remember many names ...hough some faces seem very familiar. In the second row, from right to left, are two lance corporals from ...tash, then me, Lance Corporal Tom Bowden, then Corporal John Hancock, Sergeant Wyndham Bartley and ...tain Nancarrow. The next two are unknown, but next is Lieutenant (now Sir) Vernon Seccombe and then ...geant Sidney Bracegirdle. Fourth from the right in the back row is Tony Walters, and sixth from the right is ...e of my school friends, Tony Newton. (Saltash boys also appear on p. 13.) We slept in large bell tents with our ...t towards the tentpole. I remember two other things about that week at camp. There was a boxing competition ...d I volunteered to fight. Unfortunately at about 11 stone I was just the right weight to fight a big muscular ...er from St Austell who spent his working hours shovelling china clay. He knocked hell out of me for three one-...nute rounds and won the silver medal! I had learnt a hard lesson. Then there was the lavatory with no walls, ...t a row of about twenty toilet seats stretching into the distance! I suppose it was an effective way of preventing ...ple writing on the walls! There was no privacy. You just had to sit there and make puerile conversation like 'Do ...u come here often?' My solution was to go in the middle of the night, but you couldn't see what you were doing ...n! I hope there are a few retired gentlemen out there who remember their Army Cadet days and can recognise ...mselves in this photograph.

Torpoint Lawn, 1920. This was a long time before I played on the Lawn but it's all very familiar. General Sir Reginald Pole-Carew of Antony House gave the park to the town and you can see how much the children enjoyed it – there are little figures everywhere! I remember the tennis club and the players, many of whom have now passed away. The pool has only been half completed here but in my time it was complete and we dived into the muddy water. Later it was polluted by oil and was filled in, as it is today. I think the floating wood store was later moved to Mill Creek. Across the River Tamar you can see Devonport Dockyard. The dockyard generating station chimney is on the right and the two foundry chimneys in the middle. I worked in the storehouses all along No. 3 Basin when I was a boy. There are old-fashioned destroyers moored in the river; they were in reserve or 'Up the Trot'. Things haven't changed very much.

Macey Street, Torpoint, from Gravesend, c. 1906. Macey Street, along the waterfront, was a deprived area years ago but now it's a very desirable place with river views and a convenient location. Gravesend House, on its promontory by the river, and Thanckes House on the Lawn were both owned by the prominent Graves family for many years. Vice-Admiral Thomas Graves commanded the Van Division at the Battle of Ushant on 1 June 1794. When I was young my doctor had his surgery in Graves House, and in recent years an estate of houses has been built in that area.

Torpoint Social Club AFC, Plymouth & District League, 1946/7. Back row, left to right: Bill Walker, Edgar May, Ernie Kitt, Roy Horsham, Jim Shorthouse, Ken Hoskin. Front row: Alfie Wonnell, Ron Carter, Ted Hudman, Len Yates, 'Wiggy' Hambley. They played on Thanckes Field above The Lawn and their names conjure up memories of the old days when Torpoint Social Club played Torpoint Athletic: Alfie Wonnell powering down the wing for the Social Club and the Dawe brothers playing for the Athletic side. Almost every little place in Cornwall had its football team in those amateur days.

Torpoint Albion Road School, 1949. Back row, left to right: Michael Nicholson, -?-, Jeanne Lakeman, Myrna Gillard, Maureen Hiccox, Pat Farrell, Cynthia Hannaford, Jill Purse, Leonard Sleeman. Third row: Michael Martin, Edward Madge, John Taylor, Jill Hassell, Mary Crocker, Tina Harris, Marlene Godfrey, Enid Williams, Sheila Clarke, Bruce Cudlip, Roy Acland, Gregory Wyborn. Second row: John Pidgen, John Martin, Keith Jones, Terry Collins, Mr J.H. Thomas, -?-, Alan Cook, Brian Stoddon, Keith Kitteridge. Front row: Michael Gillard, David Collett, Brian Conyon, Alan Jones, John Pacey.

Last boat from Millbrook, *c.* 1910. This photograph has appeared in a number of books over the years but I find it atmospheric and irresistible. This is the SS *Lady Ernestine* during her final years on Millbrook Lake, making her last trip for the day. It's a weekend and prospective passengers have come from all the local seaside places like Kingsands, Cawsands, Whitsands or Freathy. They may have walked down Donkey Lane, only to find this massive crowd trying to squeeze into the little steamer!

Plymouth Sound from Mount Edgcumbe, *c.* 1920. This is the Folly that was built, or partly built, in 1747 by Sir Richard Edgcumbe, the first Baron Edgcumbe. It's a pretty view of Plymouth Sound with Drake's Island offshore and large yachts racing. Smeaton's Tower can clearly be seen on Plymouth Hoe, while the Cattewater and Turnchapel are lost in the mist.

Cawsand, *c.* 1940. There are actually two villages here: this is Cawsand, while Kingsand is further on along the shore. The Square, Cawsand, is in the bottom left corner and Garrett Street runs off it towards Kingsand. Just up this street, opposite the Halfway House Inn, is a 'Devon-Corn' mark on the wall, which until 1941 indicated the parish boundary between Maker and Rame. Just over a hundred years ago this was also the boundary between Devon and Cornwall. Since then the border between Celtic Cornwall and Saxon Wessex has been moved to the centre of the River Tamar. Many ships found it easier to be victualled here before the breakwater was completed in 1841. The villages were very busy, and there was also a little smuggling and fishing: Cawsand and Kingsand were lively places in those days. In the distance are Mount Edgcumbe Park and Picklecombe Fort.

Whitsand Bay, *c.* 1915. This looks like the main beach at Whitsand with Willcock's tea-house in the background. The wide pathway up the cliff can be seen on the left. In my day we went on to the lovely sands to swim, to search for tiddlers in the rock-pools or perhaps to play with a ball. In all these early twentieth-century photographs the crowds seem to keep their clothes on! All the ladies are in long dresses and the men wear hats and coats. I presume it was regarded as a social occasion where you did a bit of courting, had a cup of tea and went home!

Crafthole, looking west, 1905. This is the B3247 road from Antony which runs through Crafthole and on to Downderry and Hessenford. Crafthole hasn't changed much in over ninety years and that narrow road with its slight dip through the village is still the same. The pretty little beaches at Portwrinkle and the Whitsand Bay Golf Club are down the hill on the left, and you turn right here for Sheviock and Polbathic. The Finnygook Inn and Restaurant is along this road on the right. The Finnygook ghost is supposed to haunt the steep hill down to Portwrinkle and I expect after four pints of beer you might see it!

On the front at Looe, c. 1920. The smartly dressed lady and her daughters parade along the front while others enjoy just sitting on the beach. East Looe didn't have a promenade at this time and the rugged shoreline was in contrast to the fine new buildings in the background.

fred John and Eileen Pengelly (née Varco) of Looe, *c.* 1981. My mother's family came from Looe and when I was
ung I was told stories of the Pengelly families of Looe. My mother was one of the 'Woodrow' Pengellys, because
r grandmother's maiden name had been Emma Woodrow and thereafter they included Woodrow in the
ristian names of their children. She also told me about Alfred John Pengelly and his fishing boat *Our Daddy*. So
was very pleased to meet him and his wife Eileen in later life. I asked if I could take their picture. Eileen was a
le shy but Alfred John was his usual gentlemanly self, and they stood together while I took this photograph.
een married Alfred John in 1928, and they used to sing duets together in their early married life. (Her
andfather owned the Bullers Arms in East Looe and all his three sons were teetotallers!) Alfred John was born in
oe in 1906 and in his book *Oh, for a Fisherman's Life*, published in 1979, he describes growing up in Looe at
at time: how his mother baked saffron cake and pasties in the 'Bake-house'; going to bed by candlelight; and the
xury of listening to a 'His Master's Voice' gramophone with tubular records! He became a fisherman in his
andfather's boat *Our Daddy* despite suffering greatly from sea sickness. To supplement his earnings he became a
wman in large yachts during the summer; this culminated in his competing in the Americas Cup Challenge
ring September 1930 in *Shamrock V*, owned by Thomas Lipton, which was defeated by the American defender
terprise. Alfred John continued fishing in *Our Daddy*, as crewman, skipper and then owner, for over fifty years
d had some difficult and adventurous times. He was awarded the British Empire Medal. He also sang in the Looe
hermen's Choir and became a Superintendent of the St John Ambulance Brigade in Looe. Alfred John Pengelly
s a very accomplished and modest man. Having read his book a few times I see a thread running through it of
ood man meeting his sweetheart, marrying her, and living happily together through the good and bad times,
til the end.

East Looe, 1906. A view of Buller Quay, almost deserted, at the end of the copper boom, as the Caradon mines closed. Looe has a long history, from trading in tin with the Phoenicians in the ancient world, to the Bodrigan rule in medieval times and the shipment of copper in the nineteenth century. It is now a successful fishing port and thriving centre for holiday-makers. The copper trade did bring some lasting benefits, however. The new Guildhall, seen in the background, was built in 1878 (and underpinned later), and the present bridge between East and West Looe was constructed in 1856 and widened in 1960. Today Buller Quay is just a car park but further down is a fine fish market. My favourite memory of Looe is taking mother for icecream and cream in Martin's dairy, in that terrace across from the quay, and then strolling through East Looe to sit on the front and watch families play on the sands, while the sun moved slowly overhead.

South Phoenix Mine, Cheesewring, near Liskeard, c. 1910. This is one of the group of mines opened north of Liskeard in the mid-nineteenth century. The first and greatest of these was South Caradon, which struck copper in 1837. This caused some excitement and eventually over twenty-five mines opened in this area hoping to make rich profits. South Phoenix Mine was unsuccessful despite three attempts at reworking; this photograph shows it just before it closed. The rapid rise and fall of these great copper mines is staggering. In 1830 the area was open moorland, then there was a massive mining boom for about fifty years, and then the windswept moorlands reverted to their former solitude.

Moorswater Viaduct, Liskeard, *c.* 1930. This is part of the Great Western Railway line to Penzance. Originally Isambard Kingdom Brunel had built viaducts with wooden trestles and you can see behind the stone viaduct the original stone pillars which supported the wooden structures. The train is heading towards Saltash Bridge and Plymouth. The mine owners at Caradon constructed a mineral railway line in 1846 to carry their copper in horse-drawn wagons to a point under this viaduct where it was transferred to the Moorswater–Looe Canal and then taken to Looe for shipment. Later the canal was replaced by a railway line and steam trains were used to take the copper directly from the mines to Looe. Finally, the little railway line from Moorswater to Looe was connected to the Liskeard main line station by a rail loop, and the line is still very busy today, taking holiday-makers to Looe.

Cheesewring railway village, *c.* 1903. The quarries in the Caradon area, on the eastern edge of Bodmin Moor, also used the mineral railway to deliver their granite to Looe for shipment, and one branch of the line terminated at Cheesewring quarry. It takes its name from the remarkable pile of granite blocks called 'The Cheesewring' that stands over the quarry. This photograph shows the small settlement which grew up around the terminus. When the railway was first built, they started building from the quarry because that was where they obtained the railway sleepers. Eventually, the mines became exhausted and no longer needed the railway; unable to survive on the proceeds of granite alone, the mineral railway closed.

Two photographs of Hannafore at West Looe. The top view was taken in 1906 and the one below in 1956, and you can see how much development there was up the hill in that time. No doubt there has been further building up to the present day. It must be many people's idea of paradise to have a home in Cornwall with a view of the sea. Joseph Thomas, a civil engineer, started the success of Hannafore. He came home to Looe to retire and got involved in many civil engineering projects. He bought some land at Hannafore and took on the job of cutting a road to it from West Looe. This interesting little road with its castellated turrets opened in 1895. He built a groyne on the end of Looe Pier to stop the ingress of sand into the harbour; it worked and became the Banjo Pier! He also built the ramp that allows you to turn left from the bridge into West Looe. The simple ideas are always the best.

...rtin Devereux, my Irish great-
...ndfather, c. 1870. Martin was born
...Wexford in Ireland in 1839 and his
...her James Devereux was a hatter in
...blin or Wexford. Martin became a
...rchant seaman and gained his mate's
...tificate in 1861. He served in a
...mber of vessels including *Bridget,*
...*rt, Portia, Conqueror* and *Calabar,*
...velling to ports in the Mediterranean,
...ica and the Far East. Somewhere on
...travels he met Sarah Marshall of
...be and they married in Talland
...urch on 1 May 1866 and set up
...me in West Looe. Their son William
...rtin (my grandfather) was born on 3
...e 1868. Martin Devereux sadly died
...ancer on 13 March 1873 at the age
...hirty-three and is buried in Talland
...urchyard (below). His grave is just a
...le way up the pathway on the right.
...widow later married John Taylor of
...be. William Martin Devereux married
...ma Maria Woodrow Pengelly of Looe
...24 November 1894, and they had six
...ldren including my mother, also
...ned Emma Woodrow.

Pelynt village, *c*. 1953. This attractive and tranquil view overlooks the B3359 road which runs through th village. The photographer has climbed into the field to get a better view, and the ladies have supplied a foc point amid the cars, with the famous church as a background. The name Pelynt is a corruption of the Celt *Plu-nent* which means 'the Parish of St Nonna'. This fifteenth-century church, like Altarnun Church in Nort Cornwall, is dedicated to St Nonna, the mother of St David of Wales. Within the church, in the Trelawny Aisl is a small plaque which reads: 'Beneath this floor in the Trelawny Vault rests the mortal remains of the Rig Reverend Jonathan Trelawny, Bart, Lord Bishop of Winchester, died July 19th 1721.' We believe that he is th subject of the Revd Robert Stephen Hawker's 'Cornish Anthem', although it could have been his grandfath who was also imprisoned in the Tower. Today Barton Farm still advertises B&B although the sign stands furth to the left. Where the photographer stood is now the front garden of the Dagger Restaurant, named after medieval dagger found during excavation for the building. On the left is Joe O'Keeffe, family butcher and groc and on the right is the old schoolhouse which now houses the Pelynt Institute and Social Club. The new scho was built behind the club.

(*Opposite, top*) Polperro, *c*. 1908. This atmospheric photograph shows Polperro Harbour with a sailing ship, a men going about their wofrk, in a boat or delivering by horse and cart. The old houses by the quay, damaged r and all, add to the charm of this little place. Its house on props and tight little streets in the narrow valley ma Polperro one of the most picturesque harbours in Cornwall.

(*Opposite, bottom*) Princess Road, Pensilva, near Liskeard, *c*. 1908. The number of men employed at South Carad Mine had increased to over 600 by 1855 and many brought their families with them from West Cornwall. A result many small cottages sprang up almost overnight in places like Tremar, Darite and Pensilva. By 1908 t mines had almost ceased to exist, and the land was reverting to its previous moorland condition. The miners w lived in these smart little homes in Pensilva must have been faced with difficult decisions. To Cornishmen, findi work was often a problem, and I expect there were many tears and heartbreak on the way.

The Parade, Liskeard, *c. 1936*. This is a nostalgic scene for older Liskeard residents, with the memorial, the Fountain Hotel, and the grand ivy-covered mansion on the right. Road traffic is starting to build up and there are many lovely old cars in the square.

The Parade, Liskeard, *c. 1956*. In this view we can identify the White Horse Inn on the left and the Empire fruit shop, both of which are still in business, now with the Royal Café between them. Stone's Restaurant at the end is a pizza restaurant today. The Fountain Hotel is still there, as it is today, but the mansion has lost its ivy and the front is painted in two colours indicating different ownership. Today the right-hand half of this building has disappeared, presumably to widen Greenbank Road and allow a better flow of traffic. In 1956 there were even more cars of a different vintage: there's a bulbous-backed Standard Vanguard, a Morris Minor, a few Fords, and a Morris Series E. When I was last in the square workmen were restructuring it and there were wire barriers everywhere.

CHAPTER TWO

NORTH CORNWALL

Coads Green village, c. 1909. The little boy in the road is Samuel Baker, aged seven. This small village is 7 miles from Launceston and 6½ miles from Callington. It began to grow in the early nineteenth century and the name Coad's Green is thought to have derived from a Mr Coad who owned land, or 'Green', hereabouts.

The Square, Launceston, *c.* 1936. A butter market once occupied the middle of this square and there was some disquiet when it was taken down and replaced by this war memorial, which was unveiled on Sunday 30 October 1921. From the left are Fitze & Son, The Joy Shop, Midland Bank and, further down, the International Stores. The bus on the right is going to Plymouth, and there is a galaxy of old Ford, Morris and Wolseley cars. This is an interesting view of the square, and just within living memory.

The Square, Launceston, 1999. I wanted to observe any changes in the square in over sixty years. So with the very kind cooperation of the management of the White Hart Hotel, and some cheek on my part, I took this photograph through a bedroom window! We all do daft things sometimes. The shops then were Boots the chemist, Findleys newsagents, the Midland Bank, TSB, Currys and Gateway. Nothing really has changed except for the modern cars parked in the rain.

Dr Charles Causley CBE, of Launceston, 1987. I have been a fan of Charles Causley, our most famous Cornish poet, since I read 'Timothy Winters' many years ago. So I went along to his poetry reading in the Royal West of England Academy in Bristol on Thursday 11 July 1991. Wendy Cope, the feminist poet with a comic wit, was also performing. By chance I met Leslie Crowther and his wife Jean in the audience, and we enjoyed the readings of both poets immensely. Subsequently, I met Charles Causley and he signed my copy of his book *A Field of Vision*. I don't meet celebrities normally, and my main impression was that they were all very pleasant and unassuming people. Subsequently I was very saddened when Leslie Crowther had his car accident, and finally succumbed to his injuries.

St Stephens, Launceston, *c.* 1904. This is a view of Launceston from St Stephens Hill, looking south down the hill in the foreground to Newport, and to the tower of St Mary Magdelen Church and Launceston Castle on the hill beyond. St Stephens is the original site of the town, and according to an old rhyme, 'St Stephens was a market town when Launceston was a fuzzy down'.

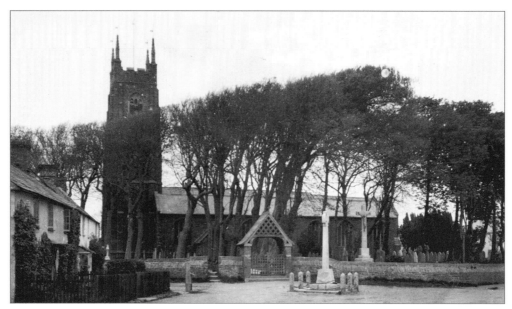

Kilkhampton Church, near Bude, *c.* 1930. This is an interesting photograph of this fine church, its lychgate, the war memorial and the pretty cottages on the left, all shaded by those tall trees running across the picture. The church was built mainly in the late fifteenth century and its patron saint is St James, the brother of St John the Evangelist. The porch has an ancient Norman doorway which is an architectural treasure, and the church also boasts many more imposing features and ornaments. The church is associated with the famous Grenville family who lived locally. On the south side of the church is the Grenville Chapel, and there are three windows portraying members of the family, and a monument to Sir Bevil Grenville who was killed at the Battle of Lansdown, near Bath, in 1643. The fine Grenville home at Stowe was built in 1680 and destroyed by a descendant in 1719.

Poughill village, near Bude, 1912. Poughill is a very beautiful village with attractive rose- and honeysuckle-covered thatched cottages which have been painted and photographed many times through the years. The church in the background is dedicated to St Olaf and the building is mainly fifteenth century. It is noted for its two unique fifteenth-century murals of St Christopher which lay hidden for many years under layers of whitewash.

merleaze Beach, Bude, pictured in about 1910 (above) and about 1950. Observe the changes that have
rred in the mean time. The top view shows the local band playing by the Beach tea rooms and everyone
ying the beach and its facilities. In the bottom view the Westcliff Hotel has appeared on the skyline and a new
h café has been built, in a different position it seems. More beach huts have been provided all along
merleaze Sands and there are more people on the beach.

The River Neet and Nanny Moore's Bridge, Bude, *c.* 1904. An Edwardian family has posed in the foreground to round off this lovely view of the River Neet running through Bude, with Nanny Moore's Bridge and The Strand in the distance. The bridge was formerly called Bude Bridge and dates from 1589 when it was part of a mill. It is now named Nanny Moore's Bridge after a beach attendant or 'dipper' who once lived in a cottage nearby. In 1643 the Royalists won a skirmish here against the Parliamentarians before the Battle of Stratton. The Strand hasn't changed much over the years but the wasteland on the right became recreation fields in 1924. I think the building on the right is the Central Methodist Church, built in 1878–80.

Church and Castle, Bude, 1904. This is a rather dark photograph but I have included it because it shows some interesting features. On the right are the houses beside the Bude Canal and in the foreground the River Neet winds its way up to Nanny Moore's Bridge and The Strand. In the centre is The Castle, the splendid home constructed by the Cornish inventor Sir Goldsworthy Gurney (1793–1875). He was one of the pioneers of steam locomotion in England and was a friend of Richard Trevithick and Robert Stephenson. On the left is the parish church of St Michael and All Angels which was built in 1834–5 by the Lord of the Manor, Sir Thomas Dyke Acland (1787–1871), as a gift to the people of Bude. The building in the distance on the right must be Efford Down House.

e canal and harbour, Bude, *c.* 1903. This is the view towards the sea-lock at the entrance to the canal basin, th Bude breakwater and harbour on the right. In 1774 there was a proposal for a canal to link the Bristol and glish Channels from Bude to Calstock by way of the River Tamar. Eventually the Bude Harbour & Canal mpany was formed in 1819 with many local gentry and business people involved. The intention was to carry de sand, which has a high calcium carbonate content, to inland farms to neutralise and condition the acid soil. addition the canal was to be used to transport Welsh coal, stone and lime, etc. James Green, who had worked der John Rennie, was appointed Engineer, and his first objectives were to build a southern canal alongside the mar to Druxton, 3 miles north of Launceston, and to build an eastern canal to Blagdonmoor Wharf near ldsworthy. Work started with great ceremony on 23 July 1819 and the canal opened on 8 July 1823. The nal had six inclined planes, at Marhamchurch, Hobbacott, Vealand, Merrifield, Tamerton and Bridgetown, ere wooden tub-boats with small wheels were lifted up or down by hydraulic power supplied by waterwheels d endless chains running over winding drums. The biggest and most ingenious was at Hobbacott where the b-boats were raised 225 ft in a distance of 935 ft. Uniquely, it employed two large wells at the top with 10 ft ameter buckets which dropped down to pull the tub-boat up the plane. The canal prospered and its best years re in the 1840s, then trade declined in the 1850s and 1860s partly because of improved transport. aintenance costs were high owing to the wear and tear on the inclined planes. In 1864 the Launceston & South von Railway opened, connecting Launceston with Tavistock and Plymouth. Then the London & South Western ilway reached Holdsworthy in 1879. The canal was losing money by 1884 and there were moves to sell it in 98. Then, on 1 January 1902, the Bude Harbour & Canal Company sold the canal to the Stratton & Bude ban District Council for £8,000. Today the Bude end of the canal is little changed but the rest of the canal has stly been converted back to farming land by individual landowners, with just traces of this valiant engineering heme still to be seen. Enterprising financiers and engineers had been defeated and the attractive idea of bridging e Bristol and English Channels died still-born.

Crackington Haven, west of Bude, *c.* 1950. The haven is at the mouth of a picturesque valley thickly covered with heather, bracken and wild flowers, and flanked by high cliffs. At Crackington Haven the cliffs on the north side are sheer and over 400 ft high, while on this south side the cliffs slope more gently to the pebbled beach. In the distance is the Cambreak Headland with its dramatic and precipitous cliffs.

The Kings Head, Fivelanes, 1897. Fivelanes village is just off the A30 road about 7 miles west of Launceston. In those days everyone loved to pose for the man with the camera, and here the farmer and his five children make a quaint family group. In the background is the ancient Kings Head public house, surrounded by trees and farm buildings. The five lanes are still there today and so is the Kings Head, looking exactly as it does in this photograph. If you go in for a drink you will see this photograph on the wall in the hall. A road has now been made past the left side of the Kings Head and a new housing estate built behind. The space in front of the pub is now a large car park, and Altarnun Road leads off on the left to Altarnun village.

orth Cornwall Hounds meet at the Old Inn, St Breward, photographed by George W.F. Ellis, 1953. St Breward is
the edge of Bodmin Moor about 6 miles from Camelford, with lovely views of Rough Tor and Brown Willy in
e distance. The main local occupations are farming, china clay extraction and granite quarrying. The Eddystone
ghthouse was built with granite from St Breward. The surrounding area is also marked with old mineral mines
d Neolithic and Bronze Age hillforts and hut circles. Rural pastimes include hunting with hounds, and here we
e the hounds and huntsmen gathered at the Old Inn ready for the 'Tally-ho'! This is a very topical subject in
ew of the government's intention to ban hunting with dogs. The Old Inn is at least two hundred years old and is
lively social centre today. There used to be a cattle and sheep market here in the old days. The church in the
ckground is St Breward's parish church which is dedicated to St Branwalader ('Raven Lord'), from which is
rived the name St Breward. George W.F. Ellis, the photographer, was born in Middlesex in about 1900 and
came an engineer, but the slump in the 1920s prompted him to try his luck as a freelance photographer. In
)39 he was appointed the first staff photographer ever employed by the *Cornish Guardian* newspaper, which was
inted in Bodmin. However, in August 1940 he was made redundant and started his own photography business
Bodmin. He supplied Cornish newspapers with photographs and produced postcards, and described himself as
ornwall's leading press photographer'. Most of his cards show scenes within about 25 miles of Bodmin. He
oduced many series of high-quality cards on subjects as diverse as china clay, railways, events and hunting, and
liked to photograph waves on the seashore, even though one wave seems very much like any other! George W.F.
is died on 4 October 1985. His photographs from 1940 to 1980 provide a fine record of Cornwall during that
riod.

Altarnun, *c.* 1935. This peaceful village scene remains the same today, except for the removal of some trees and bushes around the graveyard. The cottages, hump-back bridge, river and beautiful church still provide a feeling of permanency. The name Altarnun should really be 'Altarnon' because it means the altar of St Non (or Nonna), the mother of St David of Wales. She was one of the sixth-century Celtic missionaries who passed through Cornwall on their way to Europe. This church, like Pelynt Church which was also on the missionaries' route, is dedicated to St Nonna. The present church was built in the early fifteenth century and is known as 'the cathedral of the moors'.

Jamaica Inn on Bodmin Moor, photographed by George W.F. Ellis, *c.* 1940. This is an unusual view of the famous slate-hung, eighteenth-century smugglers' inn which inspired Daphne du Maurier's novel.

At Jamaica Inn, 1956. This is a family photograph which normally hangs in our dining room. I have included it as it shows a typical day out with Mum and Dad. We went on a charabanc trip to Jamaica Inn and Dozmary Pool, and I handed my camera to someone to take this photograph. The fierce smuggler glares down with his one eye, and Dad looks the part with his tie, cigarette and dark glasses. Pam and Mum have come out very well, and I just grin and fold my arms.

Boscastle Harbour. The top photograph is dated *c.* 1900 and gives a good view of the sixteenth-century Wellington Hotel with its castellated styling. Also notice the fine buildings clinging to the cliff alongside the road on the right, which zigzags its way down to the hotel. If you walk up the Old Hill alongside the hotel you get to Boscastle village in the distance. The Wellington at Boscastle is one of the oldest coaching inns in North Cornwall, and Boscastle relied upon horse-drawn coaches right up to the 1920s. The lower view of Boscastle shows the old breakwater built by Richard Grenville in 1584, with the Valency Valley sweeping away in the background. Thomas Hardy came here as a young architect to work on St Juliot's Church and married Emma, the rector's sister-in-law. This photograph could be very old because I cannot see the castellated part of the Wellington Hotel or any of those fine houses clinging to the cliff. But perhaps they are just out of sight around the corner. This is the joy of trying to date old photographs.

Boscastle village, *c.* 1908. Just a short walk up the Old Hill alongside the Wellington Hotel and you come to this scene. Well, you would if you were a clever (or lucky) photographer in 1908. He has found two beautiful children, a cobbler at his doorway, a man on a horse, heaps of horse manure, some onlookers and that lovely flag-stoned street disappearing down the hill. Marvellous! I expect he sold thousands of copies of this view. I hoped to take a 'Now and Then' picture and came to the same spot, but soon changed my mind. The street is still pretty but the trees now cover the Old School House on the left and parked cars are no substitute for children and piles of horse manure.

The cliffs at Bossiney, *c.* 1920. Just north of Tintagel is the little hamlet of Bossiney which once was a borough and returned two Members of Parliament. A path leads down to Bosinney Haven to reach the beaches and the much-featured Elephant Rock. This is a view of the rugged coast from Bossiney cliffs, with three warmly wrapped walkers having a rest in this lovely place.

The market-place, Camelford, *c.* 1950. This pretty little street is actually part of the busy A39 'Atlantic Highwa
through the town! In the distance, the building with a clock-tower is the elegant Town Hall, and all tho
businesses flourish in a jumble of quaint displays and advertisments for 'Players Please', 'St Julien Tobacco' a
'Gold Flake'. The Town Hall is still there, and now incorporates a library and an office for Age Concern, and ha
camel on top of the weathervane. The trees are a little bigger and the shop and café have changed hands. Now i
Oscar's Restaurant and Market Place Store. On the other side of the road, out of view, is the Masons Arms (whi
serves a great chicken curry) and the Methodist Church. Camelford is on the River Camel, a fast-flowing strea
that passes under the road. The little town was made a Free Borough in 1259 by Henry III. It was also a 'Rott
Borough' which returned two Members of Parliament until 1832. One of them was the Earl of Darlington w
gave his name to the eighteenth-century Darlington Inn further along the road. Arthurian enthusiasts suppo
that Camelford derived its name from Camelot, the legendary seat of King Arthur, but there is no evidence
support this belief. The tourists like a little mystery though, and it's always a good subject for discussion.

(*Opposite*) The Old Post Office, Tintagel, *c.* 1950. The original name of this building is not recorded but it is a sm
manor house dating from the fourteenth century. It is an interesting and rare survival of a domestic dwelling
Cornwall. The increase in postal traffic after the introduction of Sir Rowland Hill's Penny Postage in 1840 led t
General Post Office to establish a letter receiving office in Tintagel in 1844 because it was the most central
several scattered villages and hamlets. A room was rented from the owner of this old manor house and the off
was set up. It has been known as the Old Post Office ever since. In 1892 the owner decided to sell the building
was put up for auction in 1895 and purchased by Miss Catherine Johns, a local artist whose wish was to prese
it. In 1903 the National Trust purchased the property for a nominal £100 which it raised by public appeal. T
post room is on the left, with the hall in the centre and the parlour on the right; the principal bedroom is upsta
The roof is all over the place!

sentation to the Postmaster-General in 1948. The Postmaster-General, the Right Honourable Wilfred Paling visited sixteen post offices in the Bude area at this time, including the picturesque Old Tintagel sub post office ch had become a National Trust property. He met Mr Robert Nute who, with thirty-eight years' service as sub-master and ten years as assistant, had worked in the Tintagel post office since the turn of the century. Nute (left) is seen here presenting Mr Paling with a framed photograph of the famous old building. sequently, on 15 April 1950, Mr Robert Nute retired after fifty years' service. The Nute family had a arkable record of unbroken service in Tintagel post office. In 1910 Mr Robert Nute had taken over the master ship from his father, and when he retired he handed over the position to his son, Mr Ivan Nute.

Tintagel, 1903. This photograph shows the valley approach to Tintagel Castle from the bottom end of Tintagel village, with the ruins of King Arthur's Castle appearing on the left and King Arthur's Castle Hotel on the skyline on the right. The headland towers 270 ft above the sea and is an awe-inspiring sight. Tintagel (the name is derived from *dintagell*, which means 'the fort of the narrow neck') is said to be the birthplace of the legendary King Arthur. Stretching across the isthmus are the ruins of a thirteenth-century castle, the home of Richard, Earl of Cornwall, and brother of Henry III. This castle was built on the site of a stronghold dating from the Dark Ages (fourth and fifth centuries AD) which may have been a centre for Cornish royalty or chieftains of that time. The Cornish must have had a strong leader to fight against the Saxon invaders, and it could have been King Arthur.

Trebarwith Strand, *c.* 1904. This beach lies at the bottom of a deep valley with Gull Rock offshore. It is the nearest beach to Tintagel, which can be reached along the coastal path to the right. The building up the pathway on the left is the Port William Inn where you can get a meal and a drink, and sit out in the sunshine and enjoy the wonderful views.

Port Isaac. The top photograph was taken by A.H. Hawke in 1933 and I took the other one in the 1990s. I think Port Isaac is one of Cornwall's prettiest little ports and my photograph shows how the harbour has been left undisturbed while a ribbon of development has taken place up over the hill. There is a fine car park up towards Port Gaverne but even so there are cars parked on the beach. In 1933 there were still a good number of small fishing boats, but fishing was already in decline and only a small number of fishermen now catch lobsters, crabs and assorted fish. It's an attractive place for visitors, with hotels, guest-houses, self-catering places and a number of good pubs, shops and narrow alleys.

Polzeath, *c.* 1900. There were few houses in Polzeath at this time.

Polzeath and the postman, 1921. This is a lovely view of the postman on his pony and trap, with a crown and the initials GR on the back, coming down the lane from New Polzeath. The village is still very small but one or two of the buildings in the foreground are still recognisable today.

Polzeath, photographed by George Ellis, *c.* 1955. I think he was more interested in the incoming tide really! But here we see the holiday camp chalets and caravans at St Hilary Camp. Surfing is obviously becoming popular and people have discovered the rolling waves at Polzeath! Note also the sprinkling of new houses drifting down the hill.

Polzeath in the 1990s. My photograph shows the new houses on the crest of the hill and advancing forward. But in general there are still the same few scattered houses along the shore, with wide open spaces for the holiday-makers. I wonder whether the planners can keep it like this for the next hundred years.

St Enodoc Church and Daymer Bay, 1931. This is not a very good photograph but its scope is enormous: lovely Daymer Bay on the Camel estuary, where the Doom Bar awaits the unwary sea captain; the little village of Trebetherick which John Betjeman loved; St Enodoc golf course at its very beginning, designed by the famous James Braid, with that steep Himalayas bunker on the sixth! Also there's the twelfth-century St Enodoc Church with its twisted spire, stuck in the middle of the golf course, and once buried in the sands. The long-horned cattle chew the cud and watch the golfers play, and wonder what it's all about.

Thomas Henry Edyvane, coxswain of the Padstow lifeboat *Arab* from 1885 to 1892. He is pictured here in *A* which had grounded between Polzeath and Pentire Point (in the background) after the tragic double loss of lifeboats *Arab* and *James Stevens* on 11 April 1900. Thomas Edyvane was a Trinity pilot for twenty-seven years a he succeeded Samuel Philp as coxswain of the Padstow lifeboat *Arab* on 2 February 1885. He was a born leade men, being cool and resourceful at the helm and inspiring confidence in his crew. Certainly no coxswain hanc his craft more effectively than Thomas Edyvane. At the age of sixty he was presented with the Royal Hum Society's certificate for conspicuous bravery. He had assisted in the lifeboat in saving thirty-eight people from Brit French and Norwegian vessels. In addition he had, individually, saved twenty-seven lives. He was succeeded 11 November 1892 by his second coxswain, David Grubb. Over the last 150 years the Doom Bar sands in Pads Bay have claimed nearly three hundred ships wrecked or stranded; over a hundred sailors have drowned, and th lifeboats have been lost, all in less than a square mile of stormy waters. On 11 April 1900 *Peace and Plent* Lowestoft trawling ketch, anchored off Stepper Point, unaware of the treacherous conditions in this false she Under a hard west-north-west gale, she dragged her anchor and was wrecked on the northern shore of Pads Bay; three trawler men were drowned. The oared lifeboat *Arab* gave assistance and was also wrecked. Tragically, new steam lifeboat *James Stevens No 4* also capsized off Stepper Point, and many lifeboat men were drowned on t terrible night. Thomas Henry Edyvane had retired but he knew these men as comrades in the fight against mighty sea. You can imagine the shock and grief he felt as he stood at the helm of the wrecked *Arab* a remembered his lost shipmates. It was too much for his valiant heart and he died a year later.

[P]stow Harbour, *c.* 1930. This view of The Strand from South Quay shows an unchanging scene. Most of [the]se dwellings date from the Georgian or Victorian period. The buildings remain today, with different owners [per]haps and with some updating, but essentially the same. There are now some larger fishing boats and other [craf]t moored along the quay in the floating harbour. Padstow is still as popular as ever, and is usually packed [wit]h visitors.

[Pad]stow, 1944. A view from St Saviours Lane overlooking the harbour and showing the old railway line with wagons [on] the quay. The railway arrived in 1899, providing a link with Billingsgate fish market in London, but it was [wit]hdrawn in 1966. In the distance you can see the Camel River winding its way to Wadebridge. This is a strangely [qui]et Padstow, pictured towards the end of the war, without the crowds, or is it an early morning look at the south [side] of the town? That southern outer pier always had an unfinished look about it, and today both outer piers have [new] pieces which seem both attractive and functional. In the distance on the right you can just see the 50 ft Jubilee [mon]ument on Dennis Hill which marked the Golden Jubilee of Queen Victoria in 1887.

Molesworth Street, Wadebridge, 1902. This is the view looking down the hill towards the bridge. The street was named after the rich land-owning Molesworth family of Pencarrow House. In those days there was only horse-drawn traffic and just a few shoppers, with the Molesworth Arms Hotel and its grand portico in the foreground. Today they have had enough of the motor car and have made the street a pedestrian way! The Molesworth Arms Hotel is still there, looking smart in its red paint. In fact the whole area is now bright and cheerful, with the pedestrian way paved with beautiful granite kerbstones.

St Breock's Church, 1907. This lovely church is hidden in a deep dale with lofty trees all around. The church was dedicated in 1259 and much of the original thirteenth-century cruciform building still stands. The aisle and tower were added in the fifteenth century, and the porches in the sixteenth century. Against the east wall is the memorial to Jan Tregeagle. According to tradition he was an unjust steward, whose punishment was to empty the bottomless Dozmary Pool with a leaky limpet shell.

The fifteenth-century bridge, Wadebridge, 1920. This lovely sixteen arch bridge at Wadebridge was financed by the local sheep farmers and merchants and it became known as the 'Bridge of Wool'. Now five hundred years old, it had carried the A39 road through the town until 1995 and latterly caused a great deal of traffic congestion. Now the new road bridge further down the river takes the main traffic. Wadebridge on the River Camel is where the river ends its journey from Bodmin and the sea estuary begins. The town owes its importance to its position as both the first crossing-point on the Camel and the last navigable port on the estuary. Slate was exported from Delabole Quarry and granite from Bodmin Moor, and there was also trade in many other local goods. Coal was brought in for the steam engines, and sea sand to fertilise the soil. The Bodmin & Wadebridge Railway opened in 1834 and brought additional prosperity to the town. Then the Wadebridge–Padstow railway line opened in 1899, with its picturesque route alongside the River Camel. The mines began to close early in this century, sharply reducing the rail traffic, and all these railway lines finally closed in the 1960s.

Fore Street, Bodmin, *c*. 1902. As you would expect, there is only horse-drawn traffic and the road surface is muddy and wheel-marked. Note the glass canopy of the Royal Hotel and the Bodmin town crest on the wall on the left side of the street. This crest adorns the former Bodmin Guildhall, which is now The Old Guildhall, Malcolm Barnicutt's bakery and restaurant. Luke's Restaurant is on the left with its elaborate Coffee Tavern lantern, and further up is W.&A. Gilbeys. On the right-hand side of the road are Chapman's billiard hall and the Royal Hotel. Today the hotel's canopy has gone and there are new shop-fronts and different signs, but the street has not altered very much.

Fore Street, Bodmin, photographed by George Ellis, *c*. 1952. This is a more recent view of the street looking towards the clock-tower. The town crest on the wall is much clearer in this picture. The shop-fronts haven't altered much from those shown in the photograph above. Today the shop-fronts on the left have been removed and a building on 'stilts' takes its place. It does give additional pavement space in this area but I think it looks out of place.

Bodmin from the Beacon, *c*. 1910. This is a very rural view of Bodmin, with St Petroc's Church in the centre and houses spaced out all around. St Petroc's is the largest parish church in Cornwall. It was built in 1469–72 in the perpendicular style and has many large windows with tall slender mullions. Like the churches at Padstow and Little Petherick, it is dedicated to St Petroc, a Welshman of noble birth who was educated in Ireland and came to Cornwall in the sixth century. Today new estates have been built on the hill, and this marvellous view has gone for ever.

Lanhydrock House, 1903. This was the home of the Robartes family who were merchants and bankers in Truro. In the sixteenth century the family name was Roberts but they changed it to Robartes. Richard Robartes, who paid James I £10,000 to become Baron of Truro, purchased the land at Lanhydrock in 1620 and started to build this house before he died. His famous son Lord John Robartes completed the house in 1634–42, and married Lucy Rich, daughter of the Earl of Warwick. On Parliament's side during the Civil War (1642–6), he fought at Edgehill and Newbury as a field marshal under the Earl of Essex. After the war Robartes became disillusioned with Cromwell and when Charles II was restored in 1660 the new king showed him favour. Lord Robartes planted the sycamores and built the gatehouse, before he died in 1685. In 1798 the estate came to Anne Hunt and she married Charles Agar in 1804. Their son Thomas changed his name to Agar Robartes and married Juliana Pole Carew in 1839. He became a Member of Paliament and they were a very benevolent couple. A massive fire gutted the house in 1881 and Lady Robartes died from her injuries; Thomas Agar Robartes died the next year. Their son Thomas Charles succeeded them and rebuilt the house. Somehow the family seemed unable to produce heirs, and bachelor son Francis gave Lanhydrock to the National Trust in 1953.

Treyarnon Beach and Porthcothan Bay. Just south of Constantine Bay are these two small seaside hamlets with lovely beaches. The top photograph shows Porthcothan Bay in about 1959, with its ribbon of houses along the cliff and its beach with cars spread out like driftwood on the shore. I can't read the notice but it probably says 'No Parking'! It is certainly forbidden today. The photograph below shows Treyarnon bathing pool in the rocks in about 1910, with everybody in old-fashioned swimming costumes and having a whale of a time! Treyarnon is very similar to Porthcothan in that it has only a few scattered houses and a good beach. If you go there today, nothing much has changed, except for a few more houses along the shore. Of course, these are only two of many such places on Cornwall's beautiful coast.

CHAPTER THREE

RESTORMEL

Fowey harbour, from Penleath Point, with Polruan in the background, c. 1920. St Saviour's Point (The Peak) is on the skyline and Polruan Blockhouse is on the right.

Readymoney Cove and Point Neptune, *c.* 1905. The old Fowey golf course used to be above the cliffs on the extreme left. Also on the left are the ruins of St Catherine's Castle which Henry VIII instructed Thomas Treffry of Place to build in 1538. William Rashleigh's mausoleum is behind the castle, with Readymoney Cove roughly in the centre and Point Neptune, the Italianate home of William Rashleigh, on the right. Behind the cove is Covington Wood and Allday's Field. Menabilly, the Rashleigh home leased by Daphne du Maurier, is about a mile away over the hill near Polridmouth.

The Esplanade, Fowey, from St Catherine's Castle, *c.* 1910. Point Neptune is in the foreground and there's a china clay boat standing off Penleath Point. Down by the water's edge near the sunhouse on the cliff is a blockhouse. A chain used to be hung between here and Polruan Blockhouse to keep out pirates! The French still burnt down the town in 1456.

Fowey School infants' class, 1927–8. This is a real memory test! Front row, left to right: -?-, Raymond Holder, Frank Merryfield, Ronald Pearce, Maurice Heller, Donald Luke. Second row: ? Hambley (seated), -?-, -?-, Daisy Rundle, -?-, -?-, -?-, -?-, -?-. Third row: Joan Sampson, -?-, Patricia Williams, -?-, -?-, Sylvia Simons, Doreen Lucas, -?-. Back row: -?-, Harry Truscott, Charles 'Alfie' Barron, Ralph Sweet, Gerald Hones, Martin Clemens.

Dedication of Fowey war memorial, 1921. Sir Arthur Quiller Couch, the famous academic and novelist of Fowey, attended the dedication ceremony with a police escort. He is standing beside the mace-bearer on the right while the trumpeters sound the Last Post for the Fowey men who died in the war.

Albert 'Bert' Clarence Hones (1893–1962). Presumably he was named after Prince Albert and the Duke of Clarence. He is seen here at the wheel on the deck of a derelict sailing ship moored under Hall Walk, across the River Fowey from Albert Quay where he worked throughout his life. It is named Albert Quay to commemorate the royal visit in 1846 although it is also sometimes known as Broad Slip. Albert's father Harry Hones was a Great Western Railway guard on the famous Cornish Riviera line but he died in middle age and Albert left school in 1910 to work in the office of the local shipbroking firm of Toyne, Carter & Co., which later became part of South Coast Ports UK. He joined the Duke of Cornwall's Light Infantry in 1915, spending much of the war in France and rising to the rank of staff sergeant. He returned to the Albert Quay office in 1919 and spent the rest of his career until retirement in 1958 organising the loading of china clay into ships bound all over the world. A retirement present for both Albert and Selina Hones was a trip on the Currie Line ship *England* (a company he had worked with for many years) in 1959 from Fowey; the ship was laden with china clay. They went to the Mediterranean, to Marseilles, Genoa, Naples, Palermo and Valencia before returning to London, and a well-earned retirement.

Fowey Grammar School first eleven, *c.* 1939. Back row, left to right: Brian 'Guff' Ferris (scorer), Tony Luke, Len Brickell, ? Sandy, Jack Whitting, Derek Gatley. Middle row: Ron Hicks, Maurice Heller, Arthur Spratt (captain), Gerry Hones, Peter 'Snowball' Purchase. Front row: Arthur 'Rusty' Eplett, Johnny 'Weazer' Mann.

Dinghy racing in Fowey harbour, 1948. This lovely photograph shows Gerry Hones with his younger brother Tony, crewing his 15 ft dinghy *Cormorant* in what was probably a Saturday afternoon race in the Menagerie class. This is a collection of boats of different designs or of no particular class, and given special handicap ratings according to potential performance. Polruan and Polruan Blockhouse are in the background.

Bodinnick china clay jetties, *c.* 1914. China clay has been exported from here since 1869 and the first three jett
were originally used mainly for iron-ore traffic. The china clay trade soon took over and the owners, the Gre
Western Railway, built seven wooden jetties between 1874 and 1895. Here you can see the large ship *Cotsw*
Ranger loading at a jetty using an angled conveyor belt. There is smoke coming from the funnel and some ha
from the china clay. Meanwhile another ship passes by on her way to a jetty, and a number of smaller sailing sh
are at moorings in the river. In 1914 there was no road connection and the clay was brought in by rail,
witnessed by the many railway wagons in the distance. In 1922 over 600,000 tons of china clay was export
Fowey was then the main port for shipment, using ocean-going vessels, because of its deep and weather-protec
waterway. Later an eighth jetty was added and vast improvements made in the handling equipment. Then
1968 an agreement was made which allowed the rail link to be converted into a road leading to the port an
English China Clay then took over the port facilities and the railway withdrew.

(*Opposite*) Par harbour, *c.* 1910. The harbour is filled with sailing ships and railway wagons loaded with miner
There was little mechanisation and much heavy work was done by hand at this time. Thomas Treffry built
harbour between 1830 and 1837 to serve local mines. English China Clay leased it in 1946 to export china c
and then bought it outright, and by 1956 over eight hundred ships a year were using the port. They turned to r
transport and increased the loading capacity of the harbour by 50 per cent. Par is now believed to be the bus
port per foot of quay in the country.

nnick ferry and the china clay wharves. 1956. There has been a ferry at Bodinnick since medieval times.
re the roads were built, travellers used the ferry crossings such as the Cremyll, Bodinnick and King Hal ferries
ove around. This little ferry, with its motorboat companion, doesn't appear to have changed much over the
few years, and here we see it approaching the Fowey side of the river. Note the highly mechanised china clay
es behind and the size of vessel that can be accommodated in this deep water berth.

The top photograph shows Lostwithiel bridge and church, photographed by George W.F. Ellis, *c*. 1954. In the foreground is the Tudor bridge over the River Fowey, with nine arches, and with alcoves to let people retreat from the traffic. For many years traffic into Lostwithiel crossed this old bridge but now the A390 road skirts around the town and bypasses the bridge. The church in the distance is in North Street, which used to be the main thoroughfare through the town before the bypass was built. This thirteenth-century church is dedicated to St Bartholomew, the patron saint of tanners. It was severely damaged during the Civil War but in 1660 it was repaired with an unusual clerestory roof. Lostwithiel was once the capital of Cornwall with a thriving port, and it also became a stannary town. Gradually the river silted up owing to mine workings inland and Fowey, at the mouth of the river, became the dominant port. The bottom photograph shows North Street in 1915. The church is hidden behind the trees on the left. Those who travelled through Cornwall years ago will recognise this street as the old main road through Lostwithiel. The Guildhall is in Fore Street, which runs parallel with North Street, and you can just see it in the distance.

Aerial view of Polkerris, 1962. This is an unspoilt village, with the Rashleigh Arms at its centre. The ruins of the 300-year-old fish cellar, used for salting down pilchards in days gone by, are on the right, and there are holiday-makers scattered around on the sands. The small curving pier and the beautiful countryside around complete the scene. The famous Daphne du Maurier died at her home outside Polkerris in 1989.

China clay workings at Carthew, *c.* 1970. This is one of the ECC china clay pits north of St Austell. They are sometimes known as the 'Cornish Alps' – for obvious reasons. For every ton of clay retrieved, the industry produces 1 ton of mica, 2 tons of overburden and 3.3 tons of sand and waste rock: hence the growth of green and white mountains. The productive clay pit is seen here in front of the dump, with its associated treatment plants, tank kilns and filter presses. The china clay is washed out of the rock in a slurry by pressure jets called 'monitors' and impurities are separated out by centrifuges, and then the clay is refined to the required particle size. Most of the clay is used for making various grades of paper. The remainder is divided between paints, polymers, cosmetics, pharmaceuticals and agricultural chemicals. The English China Clay Company has devoted some research and development into new techniques for landscaping and restoring these waste tips to produce grass-growing pastures. They also treat sand for use in roads and concrete. Surely the environmental problems can be resolved in a sensible timescale?

Fore Street, St Austell, *c.* 1905. Holy Trinity Church is the focal point of the town. Rebuilt in the fifteenth centu with a 100 ft delicately carved tower, it contains ancient objects, memorials and some fine stained-glass windov Fore Street with its Georgian buildings and Victorian atmosphere looks charming, with the shops selling cloth shoes and lingerie. The local characters watch the photographer: a policeman, china clay workers, a schoolb and is that a farmer in his Sunday best? Only the dogs have lost interest it seems. Today all these shop-fronts ha changed and the narrow road has been made into a pedestrian way. On the left are familiar shops includi Dorothy Perkins, Clinton Cards, Radio Rentals, Midland Bank and Lunn Poly, and on the right Woolworths, Tan Stead & Simpson and Wimpy. In the big world of shopping there's not much room these days for the little man.

(*Opposite, top*) St Austell viaduct, *c.* 1915. When Isambard Kingdom Brunel designed and built his railway thro Cornwall he was forced to include thirty-one splendid viaducts between Saltash and Truro because of undulating countryside, and his budget had been reduced. His solution was to build the viaducts using masonry piers supporting a lattice-work of deal timbers. This sweeping viaduct at St Austell is a fine exampl was a false economy of course, because the timbers all started to rot away and had to be replaced by maso structures, as you see in this photograph. If you look closely you can see Brunel's piers peering poignantly fr behind the viaduct like bashful children!

(*Opposite, bottom*) Porthpean, 1905. The small village of Porthpean on the outskirts of St Austell still consists small sheltered bay and a number of modern residences. It is a very popular resort and the beach is packed v visitors in the summer.

A long-distance view of Pentewan harbour and its surroundings, *c.* 1905. The road and railway run down through Pentewan Valley, and Pentewan Hill is in the background. In the distance you can see the ships in the basin.

Pentewan harbour and docks, *c.* 1905. This is the harbour that Sir Christopher Hawkins built between 1820 and 1826, mainly for exporting china clay but also for trading in other minerals, timber and general goods. In 1829 a railway was built from St Austell to Pentewan harbour to carry the china clay, etc. It was originally horse-drawn but gradually steam engines replaced the horses. In this view we look from the slipway at the end of the 1¼ acre basin towards the lock-gates. Note the trestle viaduct on the right. A section of this could pivot, tipping over a loaded wagon to deposit its load down the chut and into the hold of a ship. On the left are unloading berths for coal, etc., and in the background is Pentewan Hill. The ingress of sand into the entrance channel was a constant problem. A sand-grab crane was installed to remove it, and reservoirs were built to flush it away but this was only partially successful. The harbour remained in business for over a hundred years but closed after the Second World War.

Pentewan, *c.* 1970. A view from the opposite direction, looking back at the once-busy basin and up the lovely Pentewan Valley. It is a tranquil scene, with a double-decker bus disappearing around the corner on its way to St Austell. This is how the village appears today: the harbour entrance blocked, and the lock-gates immersed in bulrushes. The stone quarry has closed and the railway has gone, leaving just a reminder here and there. This is a good place to visit, to clamber on the pier, see the pretty Square, have a drink in the local pub – and think of how it was not so long ago.

East Wharf, Mevagissey, *c.* 1920. In many fishing villages in Cornwall the retired fishermen gather on the harbourside to talk about how life's treating them, the latest catch, the European fishing policy, or anything else they fancy. In this interesting photograph a mixture of young and old have gathered on East Wharf, and along comes their friend with his granddaughter to set the scene. In the background The Cliff pathway rises behind the wharf, and the washing billows out overhead. A pleasant interlude in what is now a busy, bustling Mevagissey.

These three photographs show changes in Portmellon since 1932 when it was a separate little bay with just a cluster of houses, and the seventeenth-century Rising Sun Inn situated on the beach.

By about 1950 a small number of houses or bungalows had been built in Portmellon, and properties are being built on Polkirt Hill and filling the hill-top.

Portmellon, 1990s. Further encroachment down the hill and around the side has swallowed up the little hamlet and effectively made it part of a greater Mevagissey.

Portmellon seafront, 1957. The Rising Sun Inn is on the right and they are launching a fishing boat from the quay on the left. The danger sign is out and everything stops until the operation is completed. The rusty corrugated iron building looks ready to fall apart and there are a number of interesting old cars parked along the road, including an Austin A35 and a Morris 8. You can see why families like to live in such a pleasant spot.

The beach at Gorran Haven, *c.* 1940. This was an important port in the Middle Ages and the Bodrugan family built a pier here in 1585. Gorran Haven is a quiet little village which became a popular seaside resort for families, as it still is today. I can recommend fishing for garfish from the pier and playing on the beach. The church on the left has a quaint tower and is worth a visit.

Caerhay's Castle and Porthluney Cove, *c.* 1940. Caerhay's Castle was built in this beautiful setting for the Trevanion family in the early nineteenth century, to a design by the famous architect John Nash. The cost of building the castle almost bankrupted the Trevanions and in 1852 they sold it to the Williams family; it is still their family home. They have travelled the world to find exotic azaleas, magnolias, rhododendrons and many other beautiful plants for their gardens, and the place is crowded with visitors on open days. Porthluney Cove is still a popular beach and thousands of holiday-makers come here every year.

re Street, Bugle, photographed by George W.F. Ellis, 1947. The photographer was standing just up from the iction with Roche Road and Rosevear Road, and looking towards Stenalees. He probably also took a picture of e more popular view down Fore Street towards the Bugle Inn at the same time. Crowle & Son's butcher's shop is ominent on the right, the building positioned obliquely to the road. The retired gentlemen sit in their little ove and talk about old times. They could tell of the china clay workers' strike of 1913, for a few miserable llings increase in wages, and how they were starved into submission after eleven weeks of striking without pay. dies go busily on their way while others peer through windows or chat in the road. I presume the bridge road-n refers to Gerter Bridge, then at the top of Fore Street. Bugle was originally two hamlets, Carnesrosemary and llinis. When the china clay industry spread to this area in the 1850s bringing employment, the number of idents grew and it became known as Bugle, the name being derived from the name of the inn, itself so-called ause the coachman on the mail-coach used to sound his bugle as he approached to inform passengers and to rn the stables to prepare fresh horses. Bugle is now well known for its annual West of England Bandsmen's tival, first held in Bugle in 1912. Today Fore Street is part of the busy A391 road and the building housing the cher's shop has been replaced by a block of four maisonettes.

Roche Village, 1932. I think this is a most attractive photograph, with the two old fellows wending their wa
home from the pub! The photographer stood in the middle of the road to gather all this detail: there was r
pavement although motor transport had arrived. The premises of M. Trethewey, 'motor cycle technician', is on th
corner with a sign reading 'Fill up here with Shell'; he also sells BP oils and Pratt's petrol from that beautif
pump. The lovely, symmetrical granite cottage next door is interesting, too. You might guess that it was a fami
home, a little too near the petrol fumes, and that the cross on the wall was a reinforcing rod. You would
wrong! This is a postcard photograph and the lady who sent it had added the cross and exclaimed in amuseme
'Fancy, this cottage is a Lloyds Bank!' Look at the other cottages and see how the roof-line and the windows le
your eye on up the hill. Today, all these cottages have been removed without trace and the Church Rooms – yo
can just see the roof peeping from behind the cottages – now stand alone. A pretty bungalow has replaced t
cottages but it is here but further back from the road. I suppose it was another road-widening scheme for t
mighty car: this is now the busy B3274 road through Roche. The motor cycle technician premises is now
Salvation Army charity shop but the wall around it survives. There are pavements now with cars parked alo
the road, and up the hill you can find the Poachers and The Rock public houses. I hope the busy scene tod
reflects the greater affluence of local people compared with the situation in 1932.

re Street, St Columb Major, photographed by Argalls, *c.* 1905. This charming picture shows a coach and horses riving at the Red Lion Inn. The statue of a lion sits crouched over the doorway, and a little crowd has gathered. e house in the background and the shops opposite the inn complete the photograph. The statue of the lion has w gone and has been replaced by a hanging Red Lion sign at the end of the building. The house is still there d the shops now include the Cabbage Patch vegetable shop, the Honeysuckle florist's, and the Eagle jeweller's.

galls is a familiar name in photography and postcards. Frederick Argall was born in St Agnes in 1847 and his rents were William (carpenter) and Maria. Frederick became a photographer and advertised in *Kelly's Directory* 1873 as a 'Photographic Artist' of High Cross, Truro. On 17 October 1878 he married Mary Elizabeth Kelway. the census return of 1881 they were still living in High Cross with their two children Ernest Charles and derick. In 1897 Frederick put another entry in *Kelly's Directory* as a 'Photographer' of High Cross. Frederick gall died on 9 May 1900 and his son Ernest continued running the business. In the meantime Ernest had rried Harriet Jane Rees on 5 April 1898, and their son Ernest C. Kelway Argall was born in 1899. Ernest arles Argall continued to take photographs and produce postcards of high quality from his premises in High ss. He advertised in *Kelly's Directory* in 1926 but this time as a 'Wholesale Stationer' at High Cross. He was bably running down his photographic business and moving over to the stationery side. He repeated the vertisement in 1935 but with premises in Market Strand. I presume that when he died his son Ernest C.K. gall continued with the business because the family company, Argalls, wholesale stationers of Pydar Street, uro, continued into the 1970s. So all those postcards marked 'Argalls' in circulation today were almost certainly e work of Mr Ernest Charles Argall.

The Convent, St Mawgan in Pydar, 1911. Many years ago the Arundell family of Lanherne Manor dominated life in this area. They were the richest and most influential family in Cornwall. In the sixteenth and seventeenth centuries they committed themselves to the Cornish Catholic cause and suffered greatly as a result. In 1549 Humphry Arundell led a march to Exeter but was defeated and beheaded at Tyburn. The last of the Lanherne Arundells died in 1701 and Lanherne Manor passed to another branch of the family, the Lord Arundells of Wardour. The house was no longer used and it fell into disrepair. In 1794 Lord and Lady Arundell of Wardour gave Lanherne Manor to a group of Carmelite nuns who had fled from Belgium during the French Revolution. Extensive repair work was undertaken and it became a convent which survives to the present day. In the background is St Mawgan Church in Pydar.

St Mawgan Church in Pydar, c. 1906. The church and convent are situated in the beautiful Vale of Lanherne which is renowned for its woods. The little river flowing through it is the Menalhyl. The church was built in the thirteenth century, and the tower was raised to 70 ft in the fifteenth century. The lychgate on the left was built in 1862 when the church was restored. The church is dedicated to St Mawgan who was a sixth-century Celtic saint, and it contains many Arundell and Willyams memorials. The Arundell family took an interest in this church and two appear in the list of rectors; the Willyams family have lived for over three hundred years at Carnanton Manor, on the southern slopes above the village. They began planting trees in the valley in the eighteenth century and created this lovely woodland setting.

St Mawgan village (in Pydar), *c*. 1940. This is St Mawgan near Newquay and should not be confused with St Mawgan in Meneage (on the Lizard). This is the view from near the Convent and shows the sixteenth-century Falcon Inn, which has a beautiful frontage (out of view) with a colonnaded doorway and beer garden outside. On the left is St Mawgan Country Antiques, which used to be Hawkey's Shop; it still says 'licenced to deal in tobacco' over the door. In 1940 it was run by three sisters, Frances, Janey and Margaret Hawkey, and there was great sadness when their brother Thomas was killed in the war. Behind the shop is a little square with St Mawgan School and the village store, tea rooms and garden.

The valley, Mawgan Porth, *c* 1960. Here the River Menalhyl runs under the roadbridge to the sea. It is a wide natural valley with the B3276 road running through it, marred by an untidy caravan park and a petrol station. It is said that the Irish Bishop Maugan landed here in the sixth century on his way across Cornwall to Helford and then to Brittany. Mawgan Porth has changed a lot since 1960: the caravan site has been made into a holiday complex with apartments, chalets and tennis courts, but the petrol station is still there in an updated form. Nearly all the development has taken place on the seaward side of the road. There's a row of houses at the bottom of the hill and then many new buildings along the other side of the bay.

Cricket on the sands at Newquay, *c*. 1904. The harbour is in the background with the masts of sailing ships just in view. They were still exporting china clay and tin, and bringing in coal in those days. The Atlantic Hotel stands in the distance and Aunty Flo goes into bat. You don't need white flannels – a long dress will do – and all the family enjoy the game before going home to tea.

Tolcarne Beach, Newquay, 1936. This is one of the many fine beaches around Newquay. Up on the cliffs the Summer Theatre is advertising 'White Notes nightly at 8.30', and the beach-tents have been lined up in a mysterious way. This is a typical holiday scene with everyone enjoying themselves. Years ago the Rosecliff Mine was worked near here, and there is an adit high up in the cliff that drained water from the mine.

Dancing on the beach at Newquay, *c.* 1903. This is also Tolcarne Beach but at a much earlier time, before the Summer Theatre had made an appearance and before the building of tiered beach-huts around the cliff. The town band gathered on the sand with their music and instruments and played away while the holiday-makers did the soft-shoe shuffle or the hokey-cokey! Since they all kept their shoes and clothes on, going on the beach for a dance seems quite reasonable.

The Gannel, Crantock, Newquay, *c.* 1907. This is the view looking up the Gannel (meaning 'channel'), which lies to the west of Newquay. The Gannel begins life as the River Gannel and then broadens out, reaching its estuary at Crantock Beach. In the Middle Ages the Gannel was used as a port, and even in the eighteenth century Welsh coal was unshipped at Penpoll or Trevemper. Then the sand choked it up and the river became unnavigable for trading ships. The main difference in the scene today is the development of Pentire all along the Gannel shore.

Two views of the Old Albion, Crantock village, Newquay. The top one is dated about 1906, and the bottom view was taken by George Ellis in 1946. The earlier picture seems to show a pretty row of cottages outside Crantock Church but I think the plaque on the wall probably reads 'The Old Albion'. It would be interesting to compare today's Old Albion with these views of how it looked long ago. Notice the lychgate of Crantock parish church, the notice-board, and how much the trees have grown. St Garantoc came here in from Ireland in AD 460 and founded an oratory, and there has been a church here ever since. The sixteenth-century church was allowed to fall into decay during the subsequent three hundred years. Then George Metford Parsons, the vicar from 1894 to 1924, employed the architect Edmund Sedding to recreate the church, and the work was completed in 1902. John Betjeman called it one of the most attractive churches in Cornwall.

CHAPTER FOUR
CARRICK

Port Holland, with Dodman Point in the distance, 1936. This little seaside village is on the border between Restormel and Carrick districts: in fact, the east side of the village is in Restormel and the west side in Carrick. Most of those gardens and allotments have now been converted into a large car park for holiday-makers.

Portloe, photographed by A.H. Hawke, *c.* 1912. This is a very scenic and compact little fishing village with the Lugger Hotel and Restaurant at its heart. The headland with the pathway is known as 'The Jacka', and sitting there quietly on the seats so thoughtfully provided is one of the secret pleasures of Cornwall. That is after you have parked your car in the car park out of sight on the right and strolled through the village, visiting the shops and the Lugger Hotel.

Portloe, 1990s. I took this photograph from Mr Hawke's viewpoint to show the changes that have occurred in the last eighty-five years. There are a couple of new or converted houses at the back on the left but generally it remains a quiet village. There are perhaps a few more small fishing boats – I hope that means they can make a good living.

Round houses, Veryan, photographed by A.H. Hawke, *c.* 1909. These round houses were built in the early nineteenth century by Hugh Rowe, a builder from Lostwithiel, for the Revd Jeremiah Trist, vicar of Veryan parish church. He had them built to provide a solution to the shortage of houses in the area. They are completely circular white-washed cottages with thatched roofs and gothic windows. They were round so that no corner existed for the devil to hide in, and each roof bears a cross to keep the devil at bay: rather a 'belt and braces' approach. In her will in the late 1940s Miss Maria Kempe Homeyard provided for the building of more round houses for the widows of seamen, and they still exist as Homeyard Homes in Veryan.

Place Manor, St Anthony in Roseland, 1910. Place Manor lies across the River Percuil from St Mawes, near St Anthony Head; rather French in appearance, it is the home of the Spry-Grant-Dalton family. It was built in 1840 on the site of an Elizabethan house, which itself replaced a priory. It is said that Henry VIII came to Place as a guest of the Spry family for part of his honeymoon with Anne Boleyn. The house stands immediately in front of St Anthony parish church, which originated in the twelfth century, and screens it from the river. During the summer a regular ferry service runs from St Mawes Harbour to Totty's Steps at Place.

St Mawes, 1953. This is the 'capital' of Roseland and its sheltered position makes it ideal for sailing and seaside activities of all kinds. The town is built on a steep hillside overlooking the harbour at the mouth of the River Percuil. This view is looking east towards the river, and you can see how the town is built up in terraces rising above the water. During this century it has become a haven for retired people who enjoy boating.

River Percuil, *c.* 1955. The pretty river winds its way northward through the lovely Roseland countryside. What could be more pleasant than a river trip up the river in a pleasure-boat and stopping off somewhere for tea? The thought of meandering up the Percuil in a boat with a sail, and a few packets of crisps, an apple, and a bottle of orange squash, brings back fond memories of growing up in Cornwall.

St Just in Roseland Church, *c.* 1950. The church nestles on the edge of a creek on the east side of Carrick Roads, in a garden of beautiful sub-tropical foliage and towering trees. This photograph doesn't do it justice – you simply have to go there to get the feel of the place. The church dates from the thirteenth century with some later additions. The combination of the church with its graveyard beside the creek and the sub-tropical garden with its undulating pathway is very moving.

The Falmouth ferry at St Mawes pier, photographed by George W.F. Ellis, c. 1950. It's a busy scene as St Mawes Ferry gets ready to leave for Falmouth. Nothing's posed, yet with just a quick click of the camera it there: the skipper, the pensive chap in glasses feeling seasick already. The youngsters are in their short sle although you feel cold in your suit and tie. The gang plank has gone and the ferry is setting off across the Ca Roads on the twenty-five minute journey to the Prince of Wales pier in Falmouth. The trip gives spectacular v of the Fal's magnificent scenery, and boats of all types on the river. In the background is the Ship & Castle F with its balcony and lounge bar with lovely views. There's an interesting old black car on the quay and pleasure-boats are ready for trips up the river when the tide is high.

(*Opposite, top*) Falmouth harbour from the terraces, 1940. This view looks out over Falmouth parish church, in 1660, towards Flushing and Trefusis Point. Falmouth came to prominence in the seventeenth century became recognised as one of the best natural harbours in Britain. When this photograph was taken Falmouth playing an important role in repairing ships damaged at sea. Later in the war it was also a base for the D landings in Normandy in 1944.

(*Opposite, bottom*) Another view from the terraces, c. 1920. This shows Prince of Wales Pier (on the left) waterfront and the docks in the background. The St Mawes Ferry is just arriving and more crowds have gath for river trips. The docks were built in about 1859 and they have been developed to include the Queen Eliz Dock, which can take ships of up to 90,000 tons.

The Moor, Falmouth, *c.* 1910. The main square in Falmouth is known as 'The Moor' and lies up the hill from the Prince of Wales Pier. The large obelisk is a memorial to the men of the Post Office Packet Service from 1688 to 1852, when the service was transferred to Southampton. Falmouth Art Gallery and Library are housed in the impressive Passmore Edwards Free Library building of 1894 on the far side of the square, alongside the post office. On the right is the Methodist Church in Killigrew Street. Today the buildings haven't changed very much but the square is the terminus for most bus and coach routes, and is also the main car park. So all this wide open space is now, of course, filled with cars.

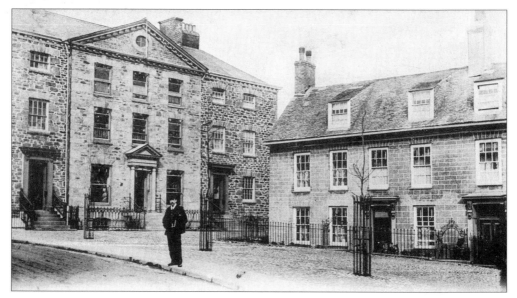

The Square, Penryn, *c.* 1906. This is in Broad Street, just down from the Town Hall and clock-tower, where Broad Street becomes Quay Hill. These two large Georgian buildings provide a very attractive picture, nicely set off by the cobbled square. Today the building on the right has been rendered but it still looks very grand. The houses are numbered 1 to 6 from the left, with the entrance to no. 4 around the corner of the right-hand building. Out of sight on the right is Old Mill House and a memorial garden to the occupants of the cottages that stood on this side of the square who were killed by bombing during the last war. Penryn bowling green is next to the memorial garden and the view from here over Penryn harbour, Falmouth and Flushing is tremendous.

ege Wood viaduct, overlooking Penryn and Falmouth, *c.* 1904. The branch line from Truro to Falmouth was
ned in August 1863 and this viaduct was the last to be finished. It is built in the economic Isambard Kingdom
nel method, having tall masonry piers topped with a lattice-work of deal timbers. So you see this viaduct in its
inal state. The view over Penryn and Falmouth harbours is interesting. On the left is the clock-tower on
ryn Town Hall. Penryn was founded in 1216 and was flourishing as a port before Falmouth existed. The
perity of both towns was based on trading in tin and granite but this eventually waned. Penryn has a great
ory and some fine seventeenth-century granite buildings. The waterway you see is Penryn River which runs
n to the main River Fal. Falmouth is on the right and since the seventeenth century it has come into
ninence. Now it has developed into a premier holiday resort, with a magnificent harbour, docks and good
:hes. The College Wood viaduct was the last wooden trestle structure to survive in Cornwall, but eventually it,
was replaced with a masonry viaduct, in 1934.

Point village near Devoran, *c.* 1908. This view of Point from the eastern side of Penpol Creek shows the industrialisation in the little village at this time. The Redruth–Devoran railway had opened in 1826 enabling mineral ores to be brought from the Redruth area to Devoran for refining and shipment. From Devoran in Restronquet Creek the ore was taken to Point by horse-drawn trams. I believe the tall chimney on the left was a lead smelter and the stack on the right was a tin smelter. They have all now disappeared and both Point and Devoran are pleasant places on the Fal with an industrial heritage.

Trelissick House, near Truro, photographed by Argalls, *c.* 1913. This is a popular photograph which is difficult to date accurately. The house was built in this superb south-facing position by John Lawrence in about 1750. In 1790 the estate was bought by Ralph Allen Daniell, a rich man with mining interests. His son Thomas made improvements to the house, including the addition of the impressive six-columned portico shown here. Perhaps surprisingly, Daniell became short of money and sold the estate to the Earl of Falmouth, who sold it on to John Davies Gilbert in 1844. His son Carew Davies Gilbert probably added the second storey to the wings of the house. The house was let to Mr L.D. Cunliffe, a governor of the Bank of England, in 1913, and sold to him in 1928. It then passed in 1937 to his stepdaughter, Mrs Ida Copeland, who gave Trelissick House and 376 acres to the National Trust in 1955. Her son Mr Spencer Copeland continues to live in the house, which is not open to the public.

The River Fal and King Harry Ferry, *c.* 1949. Trelissick Gardens lie among the trees in the foreground. The Fal River makes its way up to Truro, Tresillian and Ruan Lanihorne. The King Harry Ferry, dwarfed by the naval vessels laid up in King Harry Reach, can be seen leaving the Feock side. This ferry was built by Cox and Co. in Falmouth in 1913 and looked like its predecessor, except that the new one had a curved roof. The vessel had a steam engine and pulled itself across on two chains. A ferry of new design was installed in 1951.

The ferry, Malpas, near Truro, *c.* 1910. Malpas lies at the junction of Tresillian Creek and the Truro River. The ferryman is waiting to take passengers across the river to the Tregothnan estate and St Michael Penkevil, or to Old Kea and Woodbury. Today a ferry still plies across the river if you ring the bell and pay £1 per person. The slipway is still there, as is the gabled house behind. Malpas Marine boatyard is now alongside the slipway adjacent to the end of the house in the centre of the photograph. They run the ferry, and advertise boat trips, hire boats, moorings, repairs, chandlery and so on. Along the pleasant Malpas Road from Truro there is a mixture of established houses and modern terraces along the shore, with the Heron Inn, and glorious views of the beautiful Fal River.

Rose Cottage, St Clement, near Truro, *c.* 1920. This village is on the Tresillian River, a part of the upper Fal, a
the river is about 200 yards down the hill on the right. Rose Cottage (centre) must be over two hundred years (
and still stands today, but it now has a tiled roof and it has been extended at the rear.

Victoria Gardens and the viaduct, Truro, 1902. Near Truro city centre and beside the River Kenwyn are the Vict
Gardens which were originally created to commemorate Queen Victoria's Diamond Jubilee. Today these beau
gardens also offer a programme of band concerts and children's entertainment through the summer. The m
attraction in this photograph is Brunel's railway viaduct with its wooden structure and supporting stone piers,
in about 1850. Behind it you can just see the new stone viaduct, almost completed. Soon after this photograph
taken, the new bridge was put into commission and Brunel's wooden structure was removed. All you can see t(
are the old stone piers. On the left is the parish church of St George the Martyr and the St George Hotel.

rincess Victoria leaving Truro for Falmouth, photographed by E.A. Bragg of Falmouth, *c.* 1908. Bragg inly had a flair for composition. On the right is the *Princess Victoria* passenger steamer leaving Truro quay d for Falmouth, then the interesting wall along Garras Wharf, the schooner on Town Quay, and Truro edral in the background. *Princess Victoria* continued taking passengers between Truro and Falmouth until 2 when the steamer was requisitioned for war service. The cathedral's central spire, Cornwall's memorial to n Victoria, stands proudly over the city, but its western towers have not yet been built. Truro has changed a deal over the last hundred years, mainly owing to the silting up of the harbour and the need for more s and car parks. This resulted in the infilling of the lower Kenwyn in the 1930s and the construction of the bypass road in the 1960s. No longer can trading vessels reach the heart of the city. But we can now stroll g River Walk on Garras Wharf, and from old photographs like this we can be reminded of the city's history thriving inland port.

Princes Square, Truro, *c.* 1904. This square is not shown in street maps but it lies at the junction of Princes St
with Quay Street and Green Street, and this view is towards Boscawen Street. Once again the cathedral is s
without its western towers. The advertisements on that end wall catch the eye, but it's just a plain wall today.
hotel building on the left with the glass lantern outside has now disappeared, possibly to allow the widenin;
Green Street, and the house shown on the extreme left, now Bishop Phillpot's Library, is on the corner. To
Penhaligan House is around the corner on the left and the building with the advertisements is now the R(
Bank of Scotland. The eighteenth-century Princes House and the Mansion House are also in this street and
Victorian Coinage Hall is at the end in Boscawen Street.

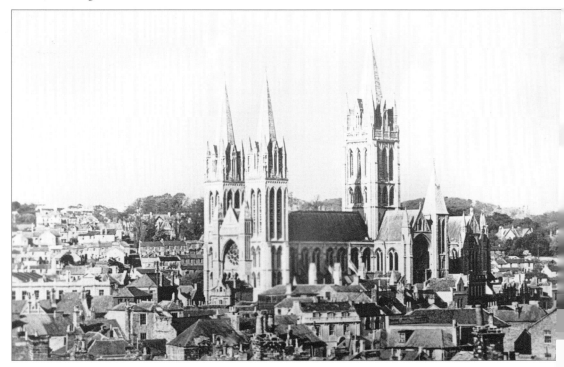

ly Boscawen Street, Truro, *c.* 1905. There is a dignity about this wide street, as with Lemon Street, ingham Place and others, with their solid-looking Georgian buildings mainly constructed of granite. There no war memorial then, no emotive waving figure to remind us of the horrors of war, just a horse-trough and elderly gentlemen in earnest discussion. You can almost feel the slower pace with the hansom cabs, a horse cart, and that elegant horse and carriage on the right. The City Hall theatre is showing the film 'Masked '. The Red Lion Hotel on the right, opposite Lemon Street, was Truro's best-known hostelry before a runaway came hurtling down and damaged it beyond repair. Its place has been taken by a Lo-Cost supermarket. wen Street is especially popular with banks: the domed building is now Lloyds TSB, the building at the end is ay's, and adjacent to it on the right is HSBC (or Midland).

osite) Truro Cathedral, 1930. Finally the cathedral appears with all three spires. This was a proud vement of the twentieth century. Edward White Benson, the first Bishop of Truro, was the driving force and rilliant architect was John Loughbough Pearson. The foundation stone was laid by the Prince of Wales (later Edward VII) and building took from 1880 to 1910. Built in the Gothic style of the thirteenth century, it is irst Anglican Cathedral to be built on a new site in England since Salisbury Cathedral in the thirteenth ry. Edward Benson went on to become Archbishop of Canterbury, but John Pearson died before the cathedral completed and his son finished the task. The two western towers and spires are dedicated to King Edward VII Queen Alexandra, and the 250 ft central tower and spire is Cornwall's memorial to Queen Victoria.

Gyllynvase beach, Falmouth, *c.* 1950. This is the most popular beach in Falmouth because it's so near the town, and it offers all you would expect from a seaside resort today. There is gently sloping white sand and crowds of people enjoying themselves. This end seems to be reserved for sleepers in the sun. The road is full of cars, although there is a car park adjoining the Queen Mary Gardens. At the centre of the sea front are the lovely Gyllyndune Gardens.

Carclew, 1918. This impressive building opposite Devoran and overlooking Restronquet Creek was the home of William Lemon. He was a successful manager and investor in mining, who also turned his hand to commerce and banking. In 1739 he built Prince's House in Truro and in about 1749 he bought the unfinished Carclew House from James Bonython. Once it was completed, William and his wife Isabella used to spend the summers at Carclew and the winters in Truro. Carclew House was then inherited by his grandson Sir William Lemon, MP for Penryn. Eventually the property came to Captain William Tremayne in 1905. On 5 April 1934 a fire broke out and quickly spread, and the house was totally destroyed. Today the ruins remain on the hill but the estate lands have been sold off.

'Pasty time', photographed by E.A. Bragg, *c.* 1905. I have chosen this fine photograph of a happy young trader eating his pasty lunch in the countryside near Falmouth to tell you about Edward Albert Bragg, who described himself as a 'Master Photographer'. He was born in the Lake District in 1877 but soon after his marriage to Elizabeth Anne Richards on 8 June 1899 they moved to Cornwall. Edward had possibly already found a job managing William Marsden Harrison's photographic studio in Redruth. He started up his own business in Illogan Churchtown in 1904 and produced high-quality photographs of all the local scenes and activities, including the North Cornish coast, the Redruth–Camborne electric trams, Great Western Railways, Helston Floral Dance, Cornish characters, mining and so on. A wide choice of popular scenes were all photographed to his high standards, and he became very successful. He advertised in the *Cornubian* newspaper and employed agents in Redruth. This photograph was taken during his Illogan period. In 1907 the Braggs moved to Claremont Terrace in Falmouth and competed with the local photographers Messrs Osborne, Opie (purchasers of Harrison's) and A.E. Belletti. Edward then started his 'Cornish Riviera' series, photographing the local area and events such as fires, and harbour views and shipping. He opened a small branch in Gyllyndune Gardens and his wife managed the tea rooms in the gardens. In December 1915 Edward Bragg volunteered to join

the army. At the age of thirty-eight he was near the upper age limit and could probably have avoided serving in the war. His patriotism was to prove his undoing because it is believed that he was gassed during the war and came back unfit for further employment, and became an army pensioner. The family left Falmouth after 1918 and little is known of their subsequent history. We do know, however, that Edward died in Budock House, run by the Falmouth Poor Law Institution, on 16 January 1928. There are several E.A. Bragg photographs in this book, and I hope you will agree that he was a splendid photographer who has left us a fine heritage of views of old Cornwall.

The Square, Chacewater, *c.* 1942. This beautiful photograph of George Potter's garage alongside the King's Head Hotel in Chacewater, on the A3047 road, is both fascinating and nostalgic. It evokes memories of a quiet motoring world when petrol was 1*s* 5*d* a gallon! Looking at the garage you can see Mr Potter's car peeping out between the pumps; its registration number starts CV6 so it was probably new in 1937/8. The car outside the hotel, ARL 275, was new in about 1934. Note, too, the lovely artistic hand-operated petrol pumps, all in a threatening row! The petrol station was a 'free house' it seems, with National, Shell, Power and Essolene petrol for sale. It must have been difficult competing with the bigger (and therefore cheaper) petrol stations, and the garage closed in the 1970s and has now completely disappeared. The Kings Head Hotel is still there, although a few changes have been made to the façade. There is a different porch, without pillars, and the building is pebble dashed. There are bay windows on each side of the doorway and a rather less benign painting of Charles hanging outside. The house in the background is now sadly boarded up and empty.

Cubert, near Newquay, photographed by Argalls, *c.* 1900. Cubert is not far from the north coast. Photographers usually concentrate upon the church which has a spire dating from the fourteenth century. I expect Ernest Argall also photographed the church and took this one when he had the opportunity. It is not one of his best as he has strung the children out like soldiers on parade. The thatched cottage housing 'Anthony's Refreshment House' is interesting, though, and the village pump, the boys' white collars and knickerbockers, and the girls' smocks show it was a long time ago.

Holywell Bay, near Newquay, *c.* 1950. There are two holy wells here, one on the beach and one inland north of Trevornick. The latter seems to be regarded as the true well of St Cubertus. Holywell itself has a splendid beach with shifting sandhills, and a local pub called the Treguth Inn. This photograph really doesn't do the place justice.

The Droskyn, Perranporth, *c.* 1920. This is the view across Perran Bay from Droskyn Point, with Droskyn Hotel the foreground. In the distance is Perran beach, with almost 3 miles of golden sands and rolling breakers ma it ideal for surfing. The towering rugged cliffs have attractive rock arches, caves and pools. Some of these been caused by miners in the past digging for minerals in the Droskyn Lode.

anporth beach and Gull Rocks, *c.* 1920. You can locate precisely where this is on Perran beach by comparing
white house in the background here with the white speck in the distance in the top picture on p. 100. Gull
ks lie offshore in the distance. This scene shows all the elements needed for a relaxed holiday. The wooden huts
the tea-rooms (and equipment store) selling 'Teas, Ices, Refreshments'. On the wall is written a price list:
hing Machine 4*d*, Customer Surf Board 4*d*, Deck Chairs 2*d*, Tent per week 8*s*. In August 10*s*'. Quite cheap
ly! People have found secluded spots for themselves and little piles of clothes lie around. Boys are digging,
ple play with a ball, and the big rollers keep coming in. These days the youngsters come down in wet suits and
nd all day skimming across the waves on their boards. Perranporth is lovely, especially when the sun shines. St
ran was lucky to land here in the sixth century after being thrown off a cliff in Ireland with a millstone around
neck. The legends say he was 7 ft tall and a charismatic preacher, and that he enjoyed feasting and drinking
and wine. He learned the art of smelting and became the patron saint of tinners. He died at the alleged age of
and we think he's buried in his oratory up there in the dunes.

posite) Perranporth, *c.* 1930. In the foreground is the Chacewater–Newquay railway line which opened in
3 and was closed as part of the Beeching cuts in 1963. Droskyn Point is on top of the hill on the left, and you
see Perran Bay in the background. Boscawen Gardens and the boating lake are visible beyond the railway line.

St Agnes Churchtown, *c.* 1948. They say that St Agnes lies with the hill for a pillow and its feet in the sea. The is some sense in that because it lies in the lee of 600 ft St Agnes Beacon with Trevaunance Cove just down road. Above all, it's a pretty, friendly village with a great mining history, and lies in the midst of the magnific North Cornish coast. By now you have probably gathered that I like St Agnes. This view shows a part Churchtown which means it's near the church, which is out of sight on the left. On the right is the St Agnes He with that lovely old car outside. This is the main village street and if you walk up past the other car you go p the church and West Kitty mine, as well as some interesting shops and restaurants, and you can also visit museum in Penwinnick Road. If you come towards the camera you see the famous 'Stippy Stappy' houses and f your way to Trevaunance Cove.

Trevaunance Cove and the valley with St Agnes Beacon in the background, *c.* 1940. There is an interesting scattering of buildings around the cove and in the valley, with evidence of mine workings all around. Perhaps the layout of the roads and the pattern of the houses took shape about two hundred years ago when pack-mules carried the heavy minerals to and from the harbour.

Vicarage Road, at the junction with Churchtown, St Agnes, *c.* 1942. Visitors have parked their cars in Trelawney Road car park and meander down to see the church and the Stippy Stappy houses or to do a little shopping and have a meal somewhere. There is mining history everywhere.

Trevaunance Cove, St Agnes, *c.* 1949. Years ago St Agnes was the hub of a busy mining district, but road transport was virtually impossible so a harbour at Trevaunance Cove was quickly created, mainly to export copper and import coal. The Tonkin family, leading mine-owners, made three attempts to build the harbour and eventually succeeded in 1710. However, it had been very costly and they got into debt and had to give up their estate in 1719. Sadly, the unmaintained harbour was swept away. With the copper boom in the late eighteenth century the Trevaunance Pier Harbour Company was formed and the new harbour was built in 1797. The harbour stood for 118 years but again through lack of maintenance it was washed away in 1915. Now we just see the remains of this busy little storm-tossed harbour.

The cliffs and beach, St Agnes, 1904. This is an early E.A. Bragg photograph, taken when his studio was based in Illogan. The beach is in Trevaunance Cove and these little figures of children in the surf are in perfect focus, dwarfed by the massive cliffs behind.

CHAPTER FIVE

KERRIER

The Creek, Porth Navas, Helford River, c. 1960.

Market Street, St Day, near Redruth, photographed by Argalls, *c.* 1902. This is an interesting view with the St Day clock-tower in the foreground. This now also serves as the St Day's war memorial for the First and Second World Wars. On the right by the tower is the post office, and around that corner is the Market Square. Further down the street is the St Day Inn. Today this street is named Fore Street and all the shops at this end have closed to become dwelling-houses. The St Day Inn is still there with a Spar shop opposite, and the present post office is further along the road. The clock-tower has been refurbished and the Market Square has been relaid with granite blocks and has smart bollards installed around the tower and elsewhere. St Day suffered greatly when the local mines closed with high unemployment in the first part of this century. It is interesting to see so many shops in evidence in the photograph; now the town is dotted with closed shops, and I expect this is due to the general trend towards the big multiple stores squeezing out the small shopkeeper. St Day is known for its impressive Gothic church which was consecrated in 1928, but then closed in 1956 owing to the dangerous condition of the roof, which was pulled down in 1985, leaving the dramatic pinnacled tower still standing. The St Day Historical & Conservation Society has recently had the building surveyed; the results are encouraging and there is a drive now to restore the church to its former glory.

(*Opposite*) Mr Richard Peters with his shire horses at Trebah Farm, Mawnan Smith, *c.* 1930. This is a delightful photograph with the horses dressed up and full of power and beauty; they are a credit to Richard Peters who was the horseman at Trebah Farm on the north side of the Helford River. Sadly, he later died after being kicked by a horse in the stables at the farm. Many years later a member of the family found the negative of this photograph in the loft of his house, and prints were made and distributed. It is a very touching and thought-provoking story.

wnan Smith, *c.* 1930. This junction is on the north side of Mawnan Smith. The road on the right is Carlidnack
ad which runs through Budock Water to Falmouth. The road straight ahead goes to Mabe Burnthouse and on
Penryn and Falmouth. The men pose proudly with their dogs and the early car, and the lady peeps shyly into
picture on the right. It's a pity the man in the road has got 'lost' in the background. The houses in the middle
ve both disappeared without trace and have been replaced by a smart estate of bungalows. There is also a little
en with three seats. Two were donated by the Women's Institute to commemorate their silver and golden
tenaries; the third is to the memory of John Christophers 1925–82. The thatched cottage on the left is still
re, alongside the road, and now named the 'Centre for Inner Peace'.

Fore Street, Constantine, *c.* 1910. The villagers have gathered for the photographer and the result is a postcard that must have been very popular. The writer on my card points out the names of some of the people in the picture and my interpretation is: 'The lady on the right is Kathleen Pargo? The man next to her is Uncle Ned Cooke. The next man is called Evans and the man standing by the pub window is Edwin Medlyn the postman. Sarah Reynolds is standing on her doorstep in the end house [now no. 61], and the lady by herself in the doorway [now no. 63] is the wife of Thomas Tredevan.' At the time of this photograph there were two pubs opposite each other, the Cornish Arms here and the Queens Arms across the road. In 1929 they both came under the same ownership and the Queens Arms was closed; the name of the Cornish Arms was subsequently changed to the Queens Arms. It now has a pub sign over the road with a painting of Queen Victoria. The small house on the right is now DAG Electrical and the cottage this end (no. 65) is named Mole Cottage. Nothing really has changed in the last ninety years.

St Anthony in Meneage Church, *c.* 1965. This panoramic view shows the church in its lovely setting on Gillan Creek. There are many cars on the shore but few large boats, as you would expect today. The walk up the narrow road from here to Manaccan is delightful, with its natural beauty, and usually a heron probing or kingfishers passing in a blue flash. Dennis Head is out of view on the right, but the entrance to the Helford River and Rosemullion Head can be seen behind the church. Away in the distance is Falmouth and Pendennis Castle.

Helford River, *c.* 1970. This is the first creek on the north side of the Helford River, and around the corner on the left is Port Navas village with its own little creek. Helford Passage is out of view on the right. Note the lovely homes alongside the river; there are many more today. Also out of view on the right are the Budock Vean Golf Course and Country House Hotel, and Trebah and Glendurgan Gardens.

Helford Village, *c.* 1904. This very pretty picture of three little children sitting on the footbridge in Helford and watching the swans was very dark on the original postcard so I am pleased to see that it has reproduced much better here. Helford is on the south side of the Helford River, just along from Frenchman's Creek. You can park your car and then walk around the creek, passing through Helford and across this little bridge to go to the Shipwright's Arms. It's a lovely part of the world and I don't suppose it has changed much in two hundred years.

Port Navas on the Helford River, photographed by Argalls, *c.* 1909. This is another gem of a place on the lov
Helford River. Behind us is the road from Constantine, and Mr Ernest Argall has clambered up into someon
garden to take this picture. Then he waited patiently until the pony and trap came along, and the cart started
climb the hill going towards Mawgan Smith. He must have sold scores of copies of this photograph. The little ro
going across the picture runs alongside the Port Navas creek and you can walk out to see the river and the oys
beds. Today things have changed just a little. The sun lounge on that cottage on the left has gone. The first sh
like house along the creek has been raised another storey, and has become Bosoljack Cottage. The next hou
Creek Cottage, has been doubled in size by extending at the rear. Shearwater, next door, has also had an extensi
Obviously people know it's sensible to build upon their good fortune in having a house in Port Navas. Furtl
along but out of view are more houses alongside the creek, then Port Navas yacht club and the quay, and
oyster farm. Oysters have been farmed here since Roman times. It is a beautiful conservation area which
internationally important for its wildlife.

(*Opposite*) The Lizard Light, photographed by A.H. Hawke, *c.* 1920. This is the most southerly place in Britain a
the entrance to the English Channel. The lighthouse station was built in 1752 and is open to visitors at certi
times. We are too far away to see the straggle of cafés right out on the point. The old Lizard lifeboat station
Polpeor Cove was long ago moved to the more sheltered Church Cove below Landewednack Village. There is
impressive tidal race at Lizard Point and rocks with names like Bumble, Enoch and Vasiler.

the Lizard, 1904. The railway branch line from Gwinear Road to Helston was completed and put into service in
87, and there was a plan to extend the line to the Lizard. This never happened but in 1903 the Great Western
ilway started a regular bus service between Helston and the Lizard, the first such service in the country. The
o large vehicles are early Milnes-Daimler models. The small car in the middle, with its distinctive bonnet, looks
e a privately owned single-cylinder 'Humberette' of about 1904, made by the Humber Motor Co.

Kynance Cove, photographed by A.H. Hawke, *c*. 1915. Kynance Cove is on the west side of the Lizard peninsula, and has been owned by the National Trust since 1950. There is an expanse of firm golden sands and giant multi-coloured rocks with names like Albert Rock and Sugar Loaf Rock. This is one of the best beaches in Cornwall with its natural unspoilt charm, and there's a good car park, too.

In the harbour at Mullion Cove, *c*. 1907. This is further around the west side of the Lizard. The tide is coming in and the lady stands on the shore in a smart long-skirted suit, anxiously watching her child in the water. Others have clambered on to the rocks and sit or scramble around. This is a simple scene with a pleasant Edwardian flavour.

Meneage Street, Helston, *c.* 1925. At this time this pretty street had an open water channel. There are two more Austin 7s: the one in the foreground, registration number XR 5771, and the open top version, registration number J 47022. I wonder how many people will remember the shops here. On the left is Eddy's before the art-deco shop front was added; then Carlyon's newsagents, advertising Craven A and Gold Flake; and then W. Wearne & Son. On the right is Gulliford's tobacconist and H.A.L. Rowe, ironmonger. At the bottom of the street is a branch of Lloyds Bank.

The bowling green, Helston, *c.* 1908. More precisely, children are playing in the middle of the bowling green, while bowlers look on anxiously! This bowling green is still danced around by the furry dancers, who then go out under the archway and return to the Guildhall. The green is also believed to have been the site of Helston's medieval castle. The archway is Grylls Monument which was erected in memory of Humphrey Millett Grylls (1789–1834). He was Mayor of Helston and was popular because he made great efforts to keep open the great Wheal Vor copper mine. The Grylls were prominent in borough affairs and four of them were mayor several times. In the background is St Michael's parish church which was rebuilt in 1756–61, as a gift from the 2nd Earl of Godolphin.

The Helston Furry Dance, 1959. A view of the dancers coming down Church Street from Market Place
Meneage Street, the ladies in their flowing long dresses and the men in top hats and tails. It's known as
'Lords and Ladies' dance, but is officially the 'Principal Dance of the Day' which starts at 12 noon from
Guildhall. They say that the ladies work for twelve months on their dresses, and the men just return their s
to Moss Bros by early Monday morning! I think that's only partly true. Helston Furry Day is held on 8 I
unless it's a Sunday or a Monday, in which case it's held on the previous Saturday. (I hope that's clear!)
streets and the houses are gaily decorated with flowers and greenery, and the dancers enter the offices and sl
by one door and come out from another. There are four dances during the day (at 7 a.m., 10 a.m., 12 noon
5 p.m.), and the 'Hal-An-Tow' song (from 8.30 a.m. to 10 a.m.). If you want to know more I suggest you
along next year. The furry dance has taken place for hundreds of years, and it's a happy time, a time to
goodbye to winter and give a welcome to summer.

Tripolitania on the Loe Bar near Porthleven, photographed by A.H. Hawke, on Boxing Day 1912. The 2,300 ton [stea]mer had sailed from her home port Genoa on 12 December 1912 for Barry Docks and met heavy storms. Her [capt]ain decided to beach her and she was run ashore on the Loe Bar in heavy surf. One man drowned but twenty-[seve]n others got ashore safely. SS *Tripolitania* suffered little damage but was driven further up the sands during the [nex]t few days. Many men were employed to dig away the sands and cut channels to the sea but she would not [bud]ge. Many months passed and they were still trying to release the ship from the sands. Then on 4 November a [sout]h-westerly gale and spring tide destroyed all their work and drove the ship even further inshore. Over the next [few] years she was broken up where she lay. This is just one of the hundreds of ships that have been wrecked on [the] rugged Cornish coast.

Dolphin Cottage and the Tye Rock Hotel, *c.* 1938. The photograph was taken from the Loe Bar cliffs looking west towards Porthleven. Dolphin Cottage is in the foreground with its garden leading down to the cliffs. Behind on the skyline are Tye Rock Hotel (previously the Rockville Hotel) and its annexes within its extensive grounds. There are old mine workings on the other side of the road, seen here in the top right corner. In the background is a glimpse of Porthleven Pier and the Bickford-Smith Institute, with Breageside in Porthleven in the distance. Today Dolphin Cottage has been extended, the greenhouse removed and a separate bungalow built at the top near the Tye Rock Hotel. The hotel has also developed its property extensively. It's a lovely location facing south with sea views – and sometimes dolphins do go rolling by.

An aerial view of Porthleven, *c.* 1945. Sithneyside is on the far side of the harbour, and Breageside on this side. Peverell Terrace sweeps around the top with the Atlantic Inn on the right and the old coastguard building in the middle. Most of the fields behind Peverell Terrace were built on after the war. Bungalows were also built further up the Methleigh valley. The result was that the pretty harbour area was left undisturbed and is still an attractive place for visitors.

ky Bowden and family, photographed by S.J. Govier, *c*. 1898, outside their home at Peverell House, Peverell race, Porthleven. Jacky and his brother Thomas owned J. & T. Bowden, boat-builders, in Porthleven before omas emigrated with his family to Port Pirie in South Australia in 1883. Jacky's wife Elizabeth Ann (née coe), the mother of all his children, died in 1896. About 1898 Jacky married Mary Ann Thomas. This otograph of the family group was commissioned to send to Thomas in Australia. Jacky Bowden, wearing the ked cap, is sitting in the front with his wife Mary Ann alongside him. Jacky's son Thomas (my grandfather) nds with his thumb in his waistcoat alongside his father. Standing behind them are Jacky's son-in-law and ee daughters: Richard Thomas, Ellen (his wife), Margaret, and Janie on the right. Margaret later married lter Trezise but Janie remained single. The boys at each end in wide-brimmed hats are Jacky's youngest sons. I nk John Warwick is the boy on the left and George is on the right. I believe the little boy in the front was lliam Thomas, Jacky's first grandchild. This is the only photograph in this book by the famous Cornish otographer Samuel John Govier, who later made his name in Chacewater. He was born on 28 March 1871 at nislake, on the Cornish side of the River Tamar. His father was a mine labourer and Samuel had a very basic cation, and went to work in a brickyard at the age of ten. His mother had died and there were two other ldren so life was very hard. He later worked in the Devon Great Consoles arsenic mine across the river. Despite unpromising start he had some artistic flair and he learnt a great deal about photography from a travelling otographer, who later sold him his business. So early in the 1890s he became a travelling photographer moving und Cornwall with his horse-drawn caravan. He rented houses in West Cornwall during the winter including age, near Porthleven in 1898, where my great grandfather commissioned him to take this photograph. Later nuel settled in Chacewater and married Annie Coleman. His business prospered and he opened a new studio photographed hundreds of groups at village carnivals, Band of Hope fetes and the like. He went everywhere hin 20 miles of Chacewater. Samuel's subjects also ranged widely, and included mining scenes and railways. a time he also had a studio in St Agnes. He became a grocer in later life and spent many of his last years lay-aching and serving the Methodists and the Band of Hope. He died at the age of ninety-six on 22 January 1967 man who rose from humble beginnings to become one of Cornwall's greatest photographers.

Porthleven Harbour, *c*. 1920. Peverell Terrace is in the background with the old coastguard houses on the r
and the church on the left, with the Bowden home in front of the church. This is before the two bungalows
built in the field in the foreground, and also before the development of the land behind Peverell Terrace. The
row of wooden shops along the front are about as far removed as you can get from a Tesco's or Sainsbury's b
those days individuals were able to make a living! Now they have been replaced with a nicely designed ro
buildings including a restaurant, icecream parlour and holiday apartments.

ⅼ Sands, *c.* 1908. This lovely view of Praa Sands was taken from Lescreave Cliff to the east of the sands. It
ⱱs Praa Sands without the café on the beach, the car park and the putting green, and before many new
ⅰes and holiday villas had been built. On the left is Hendra Beach; the wriggly road in the foreground leads to
nd then climbs behind us up the hill to Hendra, and then to Ashton on the A394 road. Today you can still
ⅹ up this little road, passing the Seamead holiday homes, and some lovely houses with names like Seahorse,
nain, Praalooha, Southdene and Stonecroft, to Hendra Beach, or walk on to Rinsey Head and beyond. The
ⅰe house (in the foreground) is Little Cottage, the next on the left is Morva, and the third on the left is Golden
ⅼs. On the right the nearest house is Sea Home, then comes Bonny Bank, Thalassa and Sea Haven. There are
ⱱ even more very happy neighbours enjoying the views, the sea air and that lovely beach with its golden sands.

osite) St Bartholomew's Church, Porthleven, *c.* 1920. This is an interesting view of the church from high up
ℬreageside, and you are immediately struck by the graveyard rising up the hill with headstones standing out
ⅼely and space to spare! Now, eighty years on, the graveyards are filled with loved ones. The church still looks
this today. It was consecrated on 3 August 1842, after the Wesleyan and Bible Christian Churches had been
blished in Porthleven. It may have been dedicated to St Bartholomew because he is the only apostle whose
ⅼ day occurs in August. The Methodists commemorate St Peter, the patron saint of fishermen, on 29 June, and
ℓ the Anglicans have their own feast day in August. Note the absence of bungalows along Vicarage Road
ⅰnd the graveyard. Torleven Road rises on the right, and now houses and bungalows have been built on the
ⱱounding land, which just confirms my view that it's a very convenient spot, and safe from the raging sea.

Caravans and the castle at Praa Sands, 1959. This photograph is full of nostalgia. Old-fashioned caravan
different sorts and shapes are parked neatly in rows in the caravan park. Dad has his Ford 10 car parked betw
the vans, and washing is blowing in the breeze. It's all within a skip and a jump of Praa Sands and lovely
days on the beach. Do you remember coming back for tea, hungry, salty and full of sand? Mother made a s
with boiled local potatoes which tasted like cream! Note the ablution block in the background which prov
washing facilities and toilets. I didn't mind getting drinking water in a can but emptying smelly slop-pails w
bit much! Today on this site there are palatial caravans with everything plumbed in: flush toilets, running w
ovens, television and so on. I suppose we wouldn't want to go back to the rustic charm of years ago but mem
has a way of omitting the nasty bits and emphasising the lovely times when we were young. In the distanc
Pengersick Castle which was built as a fortified house in the early sixteenth century. Among its features are
attractive Tudor stone doorway, an ogee arched fireplace and a spiral granite staircase of sixty-two steps.
tower and castle have been renovated and it is now scheduled as an ancient monument; it is privately owned.

egollan post office, 1938. This bold building tells the story of shops and post offices in small communities
nd Britain. At this time it was full of character with a porch and advertising signs dotted here and there for
Starch, Lyons Tea, Gold Flake Tobacco and Brooke Bond Tea. They sold newspapers, too; the headlines read
Old Comrades Reunion in London'. There is a stamp machine and a chocolate machine on the walls, and a
one inside. The window displays are interesting and the shop has all the things you find in a corner shop.
house needs a bit of decorating though, so perhaps there was never a lot of money in the business, despite the
hours and hard work! The dog just sits there and watches the traffic. Now the building is pristine, with white
around the back and sides, and a light-coloured frontage. It's still a post office with just a single sign on the
All the rest has gone: no porch, no shop, no newsagents, no advertising, no machines. And I suppose the
as died! The message is that it was always difficult to run such a shop/post office enterprise and it's even
difficult today. They can't compete with the superstores in terms of prices so they give up the shop or just
elected specialised items. Then they have to live on a small payment from the post office authorities, while
s and building societies nibble away at their business. Post offices provide an important service for local
e, especially the elderly, but you either 'use it or lose it' I suppose.

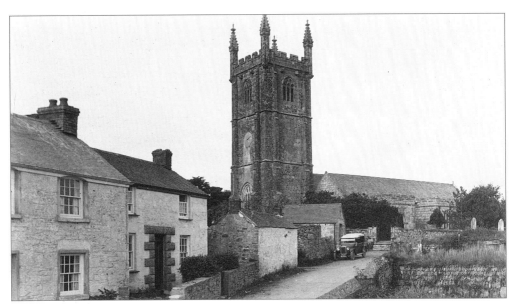

Breage Church, photographed by A.H. Hawke, 1915. This church in the village of Breage, west of Helston, is dedicated to St Breaca, a sixth-century lady saint from Ireland. Rebuilt in 1466, for many years it was the place of worship of the Godolphin family who lived nearby. In my family tree I can trace my ancestors to baptisms and marriages in this church since the 1680s. In 1988 we contributed to the appeal fund to save their murals by introducing a damp course, and the vicar kindly responded by inviting us to climb to the top of the tower to see the glorious view. The four pinnacles look very large when you are up there. This is Shute Hill and the photograph could have been taken yesterday, except for the quaint Austin 7 drawn up in front of the garage. Note the lovely cottages: St Aubyn Cottage on the left and Willow Cottage.

Breage, looking west from Breage Church tower, photographed by Ernest Argall in 1918. How did he get permission to go up the tower, I wonder? There is very little apparent change between 1918 and today. The road on the left, disappearing in the distance towards Ashton, is the A394 road between Helston and Penzance. The little line of houses alongside the road is Vicarage Row and in the distance on the left, and at right angles to the road, is Troon Row, a group of tinners' cottages. The road running off the main road and across the picture is Higher Road. I expect local residents will be able to detect changes to the houses but I shall not attempt to do so. Today the green fields are still there, with the addition of Trevenen Cross Nursery and Garden Centre roughly opposite Troon Row.

Breage, looking north from Breage church tower, 1918. Ernest Argall also took this interesting picture. The road on the left is the minor road to Trew, Carleen, Godolphin Cross and Townshend. Set square in the front is Breage House, with its large walled garden and out-buildings. Observe also the open field alongside the wall of the house. If you look carefully, right at the front of the picture is the roof of a building: this is the Queen's Arms which dates from the fifteenth century. In the background and across the picture is Bakers Row, running at right angles to the road, and with fine south-facing back gardens. Behind Bakers Row is Reppersfield Row, and Fowlfield Road is across the road. In the distance the countryside rolls along towards St Ives Bay.

Breage, looking north from Breage church tower, 1988. This is one of my own photographs and evidently I was more concerned with the Queen's Arms (landlord Mr Alec Robertson) and wondering whether it would be open when I got down. Breage House is now Breage Residential Home, owned by Mr and Mrs H. Ring, and the field alongside has been filled with houses and bungalows. The rows of houses in the background are still there but more obscured in this photograph. Breage is a typical Cornish village with its quiet charm, its ancient church and popular pub.

Godolphin Cross, 1902. The road from Breage through Carleen takes you to Godolphin Cross and this view. Ahead is the road past Godolphin House to Townshend; on the right the road to Nancegollan; and on the left the road via Godolphin Hill to Germoe. The Godolphin Arms is on the left and its frontage is as it is today, except that cars are parked along the front now. There were no cars here in 1902 though, but the Redruth to Penzance stagecoach has arrived to change horses and for passengers to relax in the hostelry. There has been little apparent change in a hundred years. The junction is more tidy now, with a better road surface, and the waste ground has been cleared, but it's all recognisable. The cottage on the right is now named Crosskeys, the white cottage in the distance is now Roadside Cottage, and the building behind the coach is The Old Forge.

Godolphin House, 1988. This house stands about 3 miles from Mounts' Bay, on the lower slopes of Godolphin Hill. The Godolphin family arrived here in Norman times and their wealth came from ownership of the Great Work tin mine on the hill behind the house. This house dates from about 1475; the colonnaded north front was added in about 1635, over the Elizabethan wall and gateway with its original massive oak doors. Sir Francis Godolphin (1534–1608) was Governor of the Scilly Isles and built Starr Castle. Another Sir Francis (1605–67) gave refuge to Prince Charles (later Charles II) before he escaped to the Scilly Isles and France. The most famous member of the family was Sidney, 1st Earl of Godolphin (1645–1712) who became Lord High Treasurer to Queen Anne. When his wife Margaret died in childbirth he carried out her wish to be buried in Breage Church. He was also a great friend of John Churchill, 1st Duke of Marlborough. His son Francis married Harriet Churchill who became Duchess of Marlborough, but they only had one surviving daughter, Mary, who married Thomas Osborne, 4th Duke of Leeds, in 1740. When she died in 1764 the Godolphin estates passed overnight from the Godolphins to the Osbornes! They lived in London and in 1805 they knocked a large part of the house down to make it more convenient as a farmhouse. In 1937 Godolphin House was purchased by Mr S.E. Schofield and he and his family have cherished it to this day.

TEHIDY HOUSE.

ly House, near Redruth, the home of the Basset family, photographed by E.A. Bragg of Illogan, 1903. This is
outh terrace with the conservatory on the left, drawing-room in the centre, and library on the right. Tehidy
is in the foreground. You can just see the east front of the building with the statue of Flora surmounting it,
Basset coat of arms and the large carriage porch. The house was built between 1734 and 1739 by John
arves Basset. It was rebuilt in 1861–3 by John Francis Basset, a cousin who inherited the estates, at a cost of
1,000; he produced one of the finest modern buildings in the country. The Bassets were Normans who arrived
William the Conqueror, and then stayed as powerful 'mineral lords' of the district. Their money came from
ership of mines at Pool, Dolcoath, and South Frances, which produced vast quantities of copper and tin. They
intermarried with other wealthy families including the Pendarves, Hawkins, St Aubyns, Rogers, Trelawnys,
lphins and Lemons. When John Francis Basset died in February 1869 his brother Arthur succeeded to the
es, but held them for only thirteen months before committing suicide in an asylum in London. Despite all this
h the spectre of madness hung over the family. Arthur's brother Gustavus succeeded him. An invalid
ned to a bath-chair, he shattered the family's previous good relations with mine managers by demanding
money from Dolcoath when the mine was struggling to survive. He also upset the local population by
icting their access to his cliff lands. Gustavus married Charlotte Mary and when he died in 1888 he was
eeded by his son Arthur Francis, who some believe was adopted. Arthur followed his father's policy of
nding more money from the mines on his lands and the local press and politicians condemned him as a
pire Lord'. He had lost local respect and his income was decreasing as the mines failed. Arthur meanwhile
ved a lavish lifestyle as a racehorse owner and gambler. Tehidy deteriorated and he sold off outlying lands.
ly, the mansion was vacated in 1915 and the estate was sold house by house, and farm by farm. The Bassets
gone after seven hundred years. Arthur Basset moved to his property at Henley Manor, Crewkerne. The bulk
e estate was purchased by a London syndicate who offered the mansion to Sir Arthur Carkeek for a nominal
of £10,000 for use as a chest hospital, and the money was raised by public subscription in 1918. By January
the hospital was nearly ready and the first patients had been admitted. On 25 February 1919 a fire broke
and the great house was destroyed; the wonderful rooms were lost in the inferno. By January 1922 the
sion had been rebuilt, with ancillary wards added; the hospital reopened and continued to expand over the
years.

Basset Street, Camborne, photographed by E.A. Bragg, 1904. In the foreground is the Passmore Edwards Library before the Richard Trevithick Memorial was positioned outside on 24 April 1933. The street was named after the Basset family but this elegant building was one of about fifty libraries, public buildings and hospitals provided for the Cornish people by the public benefactor John Passmore Edwards in his lifetime. Born at Blackwater, near Truro, in 1825, he went on to great success as a journalist and newspaper proprietor. This view is still the same today, except for the memorial and the large trees on the left which now obscure the view of the left side of Basset Street.

Tehidy estate workers, c. 1899. This is a splendid photograph although I know very little about these workers or how they were employed. Arthur Francis Basset inherited the estates in 1888 and sold them in 1917, so these men must have worked for him during his period of racehorse owning, gambling and having a good time, while the income from the mines diminished. They appear to be the estate manager or head gardener (with the tie) and his staff. They have assembled in their working clothes (some still seem to be brushing and polishing). Just look at those inscrutable faces, young and old, from a century ago.

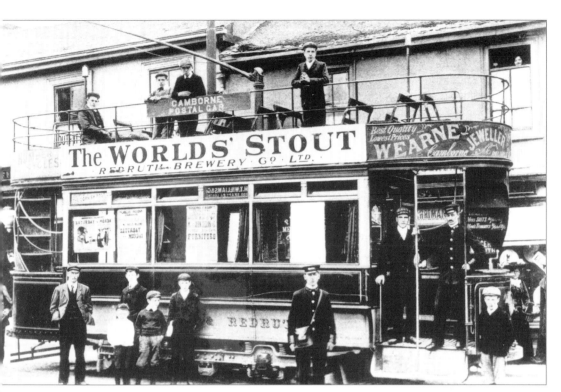

 electric tramcar at Camborne terminus, 1905. This was one of the trams used in the famous Camborne &
 th System which started in 1902 and ended in 1927. This is a postal car with a sign hung from the upper
  and a small letterbox hooked on the rear of the tram. People could drop mail in the box and this was then
 cted by postal officials and delivered in the normal way. The driver (motorman) here is Mr J. Crocker and the
 uctor is Mr T. Waters. Note the advertisements. The small ones are for the *Cornish Post*; the Public Rooms,
 borne, advertising a show 'Monday to Friday'; and John Julien advertising a Sale of Furniture at the Assembly
 ns, Camborne. The tramcar system ran from Trelowarren Street, Camborne, through Tuckingmill, Pool,
 n Highway and Blowinghouse to the West End of Redruth, a distance of over 3 miles. The trams ran in both
 tions to a timetable and there were stops and request stops on the way. There were special loops at certain
 s to allow the trams to pass, and special stops at work-places such as Holmans works, the Beckford-Smith
 vorks and the Rock Drill works. There were also mineral branch lines to Tolvaddon, East Pool Mine, Taylor's
  and Wheal Agar. The company's depot and power house were at Carn Brea, at the top of East Hill. Here
 n engines drove generators to produce 480 volt d.c.; the positive supply was connected to the overhead line,
 the negative to the rails. There were eight tramcars, built by Milnes of Birkenhead; each had two 25 hp
 ric motors. The system operated with great success following the 'switching on' ceremony on 7 November
 2. It was very popular and enjoyed an eventful existence. By 1926 the equipment was old and needed
 cing. At about that time single-decker motor buses began appearing on the streets and took many customers
 pping in before the tram arrived! The tram company was losing money and the service was withdrawn on
 sday 29 September 1927. Thousands of people lined the streets and some sang songs, but many stood with
 l heads as if watching a funeral. The only street tramcar system ever to run in Cornwall had been laid to rest.

Church Street, Camborne, photographed in 1909 (above) and in about 1925 (below). They provide an interesting comparison of life before the car, with horse-driven transport everywhere, and afterwards, with a long-necked petrol pump, garage signs and Millers Arms offering beds and tobacco! The stylish row of premises on the left hasn't changed very much. On the right is the splendid Market House and the town clock which was presented to the town by John Francis Basset in 1866. Originally the Town Hall and Magistrates' Rooms were on the ground floor, with a public hall above. The bottom picture shows the building after the enlargements carried out in 1911. Today the old Miller's Arms on the corner of Church Street is still standing but the doors and windows are boarded up and it looks 'ripe for development'. The rest of the businesses in this row have disappeared! In their place is a Aldi store with a car park (about 100 yards long) alongside the road. Further down Church Street on the left is the Tyzack Hotel, and the building at the end of the street still stands. The Market House now incorporates the Berkeley Camborne nightclub. How times have changed.

Market day in Fore Street, Redruth, photographed by E.A. Bragg of Falmouth, *c.* 1915. The Redruth clock-tower was built in 1828, with four arches at the bottom. It had recently been increased in height by 20 ft and you can clearly see the new stonework that has been inserted to make it 70 ft to the parapet. The buildings are mainly Victorian Gothic and bricks have been used extensively, as in the stylish brick building next to the clock-tower. The shop on the left sells stationery and wallpapers. It has a full window display and numerous advertisements. The shop further down, advertising Bovril, is S. & T. Trounson's wholesale tea dealers and corn and flour factors, established in 1877. It is now a Superdrug store.

Further down Fore Street in Redruth, photographed by Argalls of Truro, 1904. This photograph was taken from a point roughly opposite the clock-tower. The tower (just out of view) was only 50 ft tall at this time, with a wooden top section. On the right, just peeping into view, is Tabb's Hotel where local mine-owners used to sell their tin and copper by a bidding process known as ticketing. This fine building was pulled down in 1970 to make way for a new Tesco store. You can clearly see the names of the shop premises on the right-hand side. On the left is Jones Hotel, the New Inn, (through the alleyway between the shops), the Public Benefit Boot Co., Moore & Son chandlers, and further down, also out of view, Humphrey T. Williams & Co. Milliners, with its elegant pinnacled façade which still remains today.

East Pool miners at 'Croust Time', *c.* 1890. A group of miners having a meal deep in the East Pool mine, betw
Redruth and Camborne. This classic photograph showing the conditions in the mines must have been difficu
achieve. Some of the men are eating pasties, while a few smoke clay pipes, and a fellow on the left is drinking f
a water keg. Nobody smiles for the camera. Note the linen caps used as a lining under the hard hats, and
spare candles, known as dips, hanging from the men's jackets. Normally, miners worked by the light of a ca
stuck to their helmet with a lump of clay. The vast majority of Cornish miners worked under a tribute sch
whereby they contracted to dig ore in a certain location for a period of time, for a payment that represent
specific percentage of the market value of the ore. Out of their earnings the miners had to pay for their t
candles and supporting labour. The men and the management had the same objectives – to dig as much ti
copper as possible – and rich mine owners and managers like John Taylor and Sir Charles Lemon extolled
scheme. It was a clever scheme run by experienced mine captains and was biased in favour of the manageme
a group of miners made big earnings on one contract, the price was adjusted the next time to ensure it d
happen again! Alternatively, if a miner was short of money, he could get a loan against future earnings,
probably find himself in debt and in a weak position for years! If you were a miner with an infirmity and
children, you probably starved and died young. Deaths in the mines, and through chest problems and c
related illnesses, were very common and seem to have been regarded as an unfortunate accompanimer
mineral wealth, and certainly not deserving of a widow's pension.

The Incline at Portreath, *c.* 1912. The bottom of the Incline is shown on the right. A railway line was built from Portreath to Carn Brea junction to join up with the Hayle Railway and allow minerals to go by train from the local mines to Portreath; coal made the reverse journey. The Incline had two tracks and there was a stationary steam engine at the top to haul wagons up and down using special cables. Railway engines were then used on the normal track. The system opened in 1838 and the harbour was then very busy. By the 1930s motor transport proved to be a faster and more reliable service and the line was closed after a hundred years of operation.

Battery Hill and Amy's Cove. Portreath, *c.* 1948. We are looking from Lighthouse Hill on the east side of Portreath past the harbour, pier, beach and car park, to Battery HIll and Amy's Cove on the other side. Battery Hill is the road which rises up between the two rows of houses to reach the castellated Battery House, standing alone. Amy's Cove, with Amy's Cottage, is on the right. This view of the seafront and car park is most interesting because the Village Improvements Committee purchased this land, known as Sandbank, for the village from Tehidy Estates for £50, and started to develop it in the 1950s. Here you see it before the sea-wall was built around the foreshore. Now a concrete wall has been built into and above the sands, with a sloping random granite facing, above which are the car park and promenade.

Portreath Beach, *c.* 1920. The caption on this postcard reads 'Happy days on the beach at Portreath'. Children play on the beach as their mothers, and perhaps grandmothers, anxiously watch them having a good time splashing about. I think you can go anywhere in the world and not find anything to compare with Cornish beaches. We are looking from the west side of the beach towards the pier, and above that the landmark known as the Pepperpot or the Lighthouse. The rock offshore is called the Horse Rock, and in the distance are St Agnes Beacon and Trevose Head.

A sailing ship entering harbour at Portreath, 1902. Negotiating the narrow and rocky entrance to Portreath harbour called for seamanship and judgement even in the best of weather and tide. Often vessels would be unable to make harbour because of the sea conditions and would have to anchor offshore until conditions improved. The rowing-boat is guiding the ship into port while the crowds gather along the pier. If it was a local ship, the wives and families would wait anxiously on the shore.

CHAPTER SIX

PENWITH

Prussia Cove, c. 1909. This is the view looking east from the cove where Jack Carter, the daring smuggler, lived. His nickname was the 'King of Prussia' because of his remarkable likeness to Frederick the Great of Russia.

St Michael's Mount, *c.* 1907. It has been a church, priory, fortress and private house over the years. Legend has it that St Michael was seen on the Mount in AD 495 by some fishermen. After the Norman conquest the Mount was granted to Mont St Michel in France which set up a priory here. When Henry VIII dissolved the monasteries in 1535 the Mount was leased to Sir Francis Bassett who defended it against Cromwell in the Civil War. In 1659 Colonel St Aubyn purchased the Mount and it became a private house. In 1887 his descendant Sir John St Aubyn was granted a peerage and became the first Lord St Levan. In 1954 the third Lord St Levan gifted St Michael's Mount to the National Trust. The fourth Lord St Levan inherited the title in 1978 and still lives on the Mount.

West End, Marazion, *c.* 1920. Marazion is very peaceful with only one motorbike and sidecar in sight. St Michael's Mount is offshore on the left. Today Marazion is invariably packed with visitors and traffic. The bold building on the left is the Godolphin Arms, and this photograph was taken from outside the little Maypole Gardens which was presented to the parish by Lord St Levan. The building in the centre is now the Ferry Boat, a restaurant offering bed and breakfast accommodation. The building on the right is The Wardrobe, a clothes hire shop. Next is Avalon Art. Further down the street is the Clipper restaurant. Thousands of visitors come to see St Michael's Mount but Marazion also has a long history. It is one of the oldest towns in Cornwall, its charter granted by Henry III in 1257. It was a stannary town and for centuries mined ores that were exported from both Marazion and St Michael's Mount: the town was surrounded with mines, such as Wheal Prosper, Wheal Crab, Wheal Rodney, Tolvadden and South Neptune. This all ended in the late 1800s with the closing of the mines. Now it's all agriculture and tourism, and the crowds are welcome because they bring employment and prosperity to many.

Madron parish church, near Penzance, c. 1938. The church is in Bellair Road, Madron, and is high up with lovely views of Mount's Bay and St Michael's Mount. There was an early Celtic Christian settlement here in about AD 500, then a small Norman chapel was built here in AD 1190. The present church was consecrated in July 1336 and it was the ancient mother church of Penzance. Today the church looks as it did in 1938: only the trees have gone. The Old Vicarage is up for sale and the vicar has moved into the New Vicarage next door. Madron Daniel's School, opened in 1878, is out of view on the right.

Market Jew Street, Penzance, c. 1902. This is easily recognisable with the statue of Penzance's famous son Sir Humphry Davy, the inventor of the miner's safety lamp, standing in front of the Market House with its Ionic columns and dome. The high pavement on the right and the houses also seem to be as we see them today, but the road traffic is a different matter. On the right the GWR porter with a horse-drawn wagon is taking goods to the shops, and a number of Hansom cabs are for hire at the Market Hall. There is a cyclist in the road but no motor cars. The shops on the right are Thomas Mear, Bradbury's and C. Oliver. On the left is the Castle Hotel. The Spanish sacked the town in 1595 so the buildings in general date from that time.

Two views of Penzance harbour, *c.* 1900. The top photograph was taken from the South Pier and looks across the floating dock and its gates towards The Quay and Wharf Road. It also gives a panoramic view of Penzance with St Mary's Church on the left and the dome of the Market Hall in Market Jew Street on the right. The bottom view, also from South Quay, was taken from nearer the Barbican, with Quay Street coming down from Chapel Street on the left. The quay opposite is Pochin's clay wharf with the ship loading alongside, and the long warehouse is their china clay store. The clay came from works at Tredinney, St Buryan, Ludgvan and Towednack, and this business continued until about 1935. The harbour has been used to import and export many commodities since it was developed in the mid-nineteenth century. The Albert Pier was built in 1845–7, then the South Pier was extended in 1852–4. The last major work was the building of the floating dock in 1878–84.

Jack and Elizabeth Stevens with three of their five children, pictured at Penzance, 18 June 1923. Jack Stevens (1868–1949), seated on the left, was a well-known Penzance basket-maker; his wife Elizabeth, on the right, was a member of the Denley family who were merchants and shipowners of Penzance. Lily Stevens (1889–1953), standing, was their second child and she remained unmarried. She was a postcard collector and a number of the photographs in this book are from her collection. Their son Bill Stevens is pictured in his Canadian uniform having emigrated to Canada like Charles and James, his two elder brothers. Bert Stevens (1901–94) became a merchant seaman at the age of sixteen and joined the Trinity House Service in 1940.

Morrab Gardens, Penzance, *c.* 1906. This is a beautifully composed photograph, with the gardens in all their tropical splendour, the Victorian bandstand, and these elegantly dressed Edwardian ladies coming down the pathway. These gardens are an advertisement for the climate of the town. Very few public gardens could equal this display of so many subtropical plants. The fine palms, myrtles, geraniums, camelias and other equally tender plants thrive here all the year round.

The Promenade, looking towards Newlyn, Penzance, 1935. People are strolling on the Promenade and enjoying the view. The gentleman in the boater is a 'regular', who appears in other photographs of the Promenade. Note the sign reading 'Tidal Swimming Baths, Mixed Bathing' – which really means Lariggan beach by the look of it! The baths, with their elaborate Victorian design, look intriguing, and the Union Jack is flying in an onshore breeze. The Marina café awaits you and the Ladies' Orchestra plays. With the soda fountain, fruit sundaes and Cornish cream ices, this is a little piece of nostalgia for times when some of us were very young, and some weren't born at all.

The Cocking family, Penzance, *c.* 1904. Mr James Cocking stands at the back, with his wife Sarah Pick Cocking (née Craze) seated in the middle. Their eldest son Thomas James Garfield is on the left, and younger son William Ernest on the right. The eldest daughter (on the left) is Edith Penberthy and the younger daughter is Selina (Lina) Bottrell. James Cocking was an HM Coastguard/Royal Naval reservist as a young man. He married Sarah on Christmas Eve 1889 and the family lived in coastguard housing in St Just and Pendeen until the end of the century. On leaving the coastguard service, James and his family moved to 2 Albert Terrace, Penzance, and he worked as an insurance agent. Thomas J.G. Cocking went to sea with the local (Hayle) shipping line and progressed to become a Master Mariner (captain) with the Blue Funnel Line. On retirement from the sea he lived in St Ives, becoming first a butcher and then an insurance agent. William E. Cocking went into the drapery trade and for many years was manager of the West End drapery stores in Redruth. Later he had his own shop, Cockings Ltd, in Redruth. Edith Penberthy Cocking became a primary school teacher and continued to live in the family home. She taught infants for most of her working life at St Erth School, travelling daily from Penzance. Selina Cocking became a solicitor's secretary until her marriage in 1921 to Albert 'Bert' Clarence Hones. They lived first in Golant on the Fowey River, and later in Fowey, and they had two sons, Gerald and Antony.

Newlyn, *c.* 1950. Cornwall's largest and busiest fishing port, photographed from the South Pier looking towards the fish market and the Strand. It's been a difficult fifty years since then with the fishermen fighting for their livelihood, and tangling with European bureaucracy. Meanwhile the members of the Newlyn School of Artists still enjoy the clear light and the bustling harbour, displaying their paintings and sculpture in Newlyn Art Gallery.

Mousehole harbour, *c.* 1918. The children are happily messing about in boats as the old fishermen pose for the camera. The Ship Inn is in the background with its sign on the wall, and it's probably before the pub expanded into the adjoining house on the right. It was also before the Lobster Pot Hotel built a balcony out over the harbour, replacing the terrace visible in this view. Mousehole has remained an unspoilt harbour, largely by encouraging most motorists to park before they get there.

Lamorna, *c.* 1915. Most people know Lamorna's lovely valley and little harbour, with its abandoned granite quarries. Here we see the short row of cottages behind the harbour, and the granite foot-bridge across the stream which runs down to the sea. The quarry was in business for many years and supplied granite for the Thames Embankment, a new pier in Mousehole and the Wolf Rock lighthouse. It closed in the 1920s. This scene, with an early motor van at the end of the lane and people picnicking on the grass, sums up for me the turning-point when the old industries died away, making way for the new tourist trade.

Pemberth Cove, *c.* 1910. This delightful cove, under the care of the National Trust, still looks much the same today. The cove is at the end of the sheltered and wooded Pemberth valley and still has a fishing community. In this picture you can see the old windlass, a slipway and a group of granite cottages; today you will also see a modern power winch and about a dozen well-equipped fishing boats. They mainly fish with lines for mackerel and bass, with some crabbing, lobster-potting and gill-netting.

Porthcurno, photographed by A.H. Hawke, *c.* 1912. This shows Porthcurno before it became popular as a beach resort. More houses have since been built, and there is now a large car park. The pathway on the right goes down to Porthcurno beach with its sand composed of finely ground sea-shells. In about 1880 the Cable & Wireless Company brought their first telephone cable ashore here, thus linking Britain with America via the cable from Brest. Subsequently many more cables came ashore here, and the company set up an operating station and engineering college. With advances in communications the company decided to dispense with these facilities. They finally left in 1993 and handed over their coastal property to the National Trust.

Minack Theatre and Logan Rock, *c.* 1960. Miss Rowena Cade founded this amphitheatre on the 250 ft cliffs near Porthcurno in 1932. It was hewn out of the cliff and took twenty years to complete. A theatrical group stages productions throughout the summer season against this magnificent setting of cliffs, sea and sky. The headland in the distance is Treen cliffs (Treryn Dinas), with the finely balanced 60-ton Logan Rock. In 1824 it was pushed off its fulcrum by Lieutenant Goldsmith (the nephew of Oliver Goldsmith the poet) and the crew of his revenue cutter *Nimble*. There was a public outcry and the Admiralty ordered Goldsmith to replace the stone at his own cost. He achieved this difficult task for a cost of about £130, but it has never rocked with the same ease as before.

Godrevy Lighthouse, St Ives Bay, 1927. This is one of the many Trinity House lighthouses around the Cornish coast. They were installed because of the hundreds of shipwrecks that have occurred on both north and south coasts. There had been a large number of shipwrecks in the vicinity of Godrevy during the first half of the nineteenth century, including *Reward* (1845), *Expedition* (1848), *Hope* (1852), *Mount Charles* (1853) and many others. Then in November 1854 *Nile* went down off Godrevy and all sixty crew and an unknown number of passengers were drowned. There was a public outcry, demanding that a lighthouse should be built on Godrevy Island; this was successful and the lighthouse was installed in 1859. Originally manned, it is now worked automatically.

Chalets and post office, Hayle Towans, *c.* 1938. In the background can be seen Godrevy island and Godrevy Point. At this time the Towans were rather primitive with cars parked between the chalets, tents or caravans. This view shows it all: the washing on the line, the water barrels, outside toilets, the telephone poles – but I can't see the post office. The Towans today seem much more organised, with a number of holiday camps offering 'swish' facilities for family holidays. The main attraction, of course, has always been the lovely beach with its fringe of sand-dunes.

Courting couples and Gwithian beach, photographed by A.H. Hawke, *c.* 1925. It's a lovely day and the coupl have found a quiet spot in the Towans overlooking Gwithian Beach to do some courting – when this old fello comes along with his camera! Alfred H. Hawke was born in Bristol on 7 February 1881, the son of Richard ar Eliza Hawke. I think that Richard was a native of Helston, and Alfred eventually started a photography ar postcard business there in 1905 featuring local events like shipwrecks and the Helston Floral Dance. His fir premises were at 46 Meneage Street, which he called The Studio. On 27 March 1907 he married Miss Cla White at St Michael's Church, and they moved to 43 Meneage Street. He continued to produce postcards to a hig standard, mainly of the Helston and Lizard area. Alfred needed a car for his work and he took out his first drivir licence in 1906, and his vehicles regularly appeared in his photographs. He was able to visit Newquay, St Colon Major and other places up to the start of the First World War in 1914. Then he was restricted by the Defence the Realm Act which forbade the photography of coastal areas. In 1917 Alfred joined the Royal Flying Corps as photographer. When he returned from the war he obtained new premises at 5 Meneage Street near the junctic with Coinagehall Street. By the 1920s he was mass-producing black and white photographs and postcards of t Helston, Lizard, Penwith and North Cornwall areas. About this time he took an interest in the Old Cornwa Society in Helston, and undertook some Magic Lantern lectures with a friend doing the talking and Alfr operating the slides – and selling a few postcards! He also helped to start the first museum in Helston, which now excellent and is situated behind the Guildhall. Mr A.H. Hawke retired on 1 March 1952 to live in the f above his premises, but he still came down to help his successor when required. He died on 11 May 1958 ag seventy-seven, and he will be remembered as a man who has provided us with an invaluable record of Cornish in the first half of the twentieth century.

Hayle Towans. The top view is dated about 1920 and we are looking out across the bay towards Lelant, Carbis and St Ives. The caption mentions Knill's Memorial, but you would need plenty of imagination to see it on the hill on the left! The early Austin 7, registration number YT 3314, stands among the dunes, suggesting the start of tourism as we know it today. But nobody's in sight, or is that someone peeping from behind the caravan on the right? The photograph below is from about 1938, judging by the ladies' hats, although the postcard was posted on 30 September 1943. The children paddle in the pool on the sands under Mum's watchful eye, and the cave and the little shop on the cliff should help you to identify the exact location.

Phillack village, Hayle Towans, *c.* 1959. This is the road going through Phillack with Phillack Hill going down of the right. Phillack Church and its large graveyard stand out starkly on the edge of Hayle Towans. There has been a church here since St Piala and St Gwithian arrived in the fifth century. St Piala is said to have been martyre and the original church was dedicated to him. The Normans came in the eleventh century, rebuilt the church an substituted St Felicitas for St Piala because they had no knowledge of Celtic saints. The Norman church was turn replaced by another building with a higher tower in the fifteenth century. This church was rebuilt 1856–7, when it was enlarged to hold 320 in the congregation. There has been an unbroken succession of recto here since 1257, proving that the citizens of Phillack parish have worshipped here for a very long time! Today t church still looks the same and the ladies of the congregation have made a wonderful array of colourful kneele Inevitably, the graveyard has expanded on the left, up into the rolling Towans, and has almost doubled in size suppose the only thing certain in life is death. They all lie buried in the sand with beautiful St Ives Bay in t background. In the foreground on the left is Mexico Lane and further down in front of the car is the Bucket Blood public house. This unusual name refers to the story that a man was murdered and thrown down the we and when the inn-keeper went to get water all he got was a bucket of blood! Apparently more sensitive souls ha changed the name to the New Inn in the past, but the more bloody-minded have now restored the former name

(*Opposite*) Lelant, St Ives, *c.* 1904. This is Church Road, a turning off Fore Street, Lelant, leading down to church by the West of Cornwall golf course. I don't think the road has changed very much, except it's perhap little less rural now. In the distance is Lelant Church, dedicated to St Uny, a brother of St Ia of St Ives. It's a lov spot for a links golf course, but a bit tricky with all those sand-dunes! But there's always the clubhouse an quiet game of snooker.

ndary Square, Hayle, *c.* 1906. Twelve little boys with white collars stand on the island in the middle, making
square look very large. On the left is the Foundary Methodist Chapel built in 1845, which is now a shopping
ide. The imposing building at the end of the square is the White Hart Hotel, which is still there. It was built in
1830s as a home for Henry Harvey of the Harvey Company. The building on the right was the original White
t Hotel which was built in the early nineteenth century as a business for Harvey's daughter Jane Trevithick,
wife of famous Richard Trevithick, who spent long periods away on engineering work. The history of Hayle in
eighteenth and nineteenth centuries is bound up with the success of Harvey's foundry and other works which
ufactured heavy engineering equipment in the west end of the town, and with the Cornish Copper Company
ch smelted copper at Copperhouse in the east. The harbour was also busy in those days but it has silted up in
nt years.

Carbis Bay, 1901. The loveliest railway line in Cornwall snakes around the coast by Lelant and strides over Carbis Bay viaduct, past the Carbis Bay Hotel on the beach, and then shoots off to St Ives. The best way to arrive is by train, and the scenery keeps you glued to the starboard window all the way! Pretty Carbis Bay with its lovely sands is getting busier every year.

Porthminster beach, *c*. 1920. The photographer is standing in St Ives railway station car park and looking across Porthminster Beach. The name means 'church cove' and it was so-called because there was a small chapel here by the stream. The beach scene is familiar with a large number of beach tents, and many people on the beach, but few of them have taken off their clothes and hardly any actually go in the water. What a difference now!

the beach at St Ives, 5 August 1950. We went on a coach trip to St Ives and this smashing photograph must ⸱e been taken by Les Waldron, my girlfriend's father. Everyone's happy and smiling into the camera, and that's ⸱ I remember those days on the beach. We must have just arrived because I've still got my tie on! At the back Lilian and Edith with their Mum, Mrs Lilian Urell ('Aunt Lil' to us), sitting in the middle. In front of them is ⸱ (my girlfriend), Keith (Edith's son), and me, with Glenda (Edith's daughter) nearest the camera. Pam and I married in 1951 so in this picture you see the start of a long and happy relationship. When I started courting ⸱ I soon learned that Aunt Lil was somebody special. A woman of indomitable spirit, she had brought up her ⸱ girls on her own when her husband died young. She became an upholsteress in Devonport Dockyard and did ⸱d service during the war. When her grandchildren Keith and Glenda were young, Aunt Lil took them and Pam ⸱ outings to beauty spots all around Plymouth by bus or steamer or train. They went to Meavy, Grenofin, ⸱nyll, Mount Edgcumbe, Whitsand, Cawsands and Cargreen. There would be picnicking, swimming, games or ⸱kberry picking. Such trips were the highlight of Pam's childhood. I suppose many of us know someone like ⸱t Lil, a mother or a relative who quietly gets on with life and spreads happiness around by their good work.

Landing fish on the slipway, St Ives, 1932. The photographs on this spread show the Wharf to illustrate how St Ives harbour has changed. You can see for yourself the differences between now and then. St Ives still had a fishing fleet in the 1930s, judging by the fish on the beach. It's a bustling scene with fishermen looking on, horses and carts in the water, and buyers, dogs and dead fish everywhere! The view around the harbour from St Ia's Church to the slipway is interesting, too. Where are all the visitors, icecreams and trips around the bay? Was it so different seventy years ago?

The Wharf, the Sloop Inn and the Slipway, St Ives, 1954. The Sloop public house on the Wharf has been there for hundreds of years. Not much could have changed in just twenty years, although there are more visitors strolling up and down, and sitting on the harbour beach. The little group of locals chat away on the left, perhaps about going in for boat trips, and coming home for tea at 5 o'clock.

The Smeaton's Pier end of the Wharf, St Ives, *c.* 1908. The postcard's original caption reads 'Old Houses on the Wharf'. At the turn of the century St Ives was a fishing village and not a holiday resort, and money had to be earned, with difficulty, from the mighty sea. The words 'Quicks Sail Loft' are painted on the wall, and 'C. Stevens Beer Bar' over the seated figures. The old men sit and talk as usual and children play in the quiet street. There are interesting buildings in all shapes and sizes, a shop here and there, and a narrow cobbled way. This was life in St Ives before the surging waves of visitors.

The Smeaton's Pier end of the Wharf, St Ives, 1990s. This is my photograph of what I think is the same part of the Wharf. You will not need me to point out all the changes. In general, though, the thoroughfare has been widened and the owners of these properties have, very sensibly, made the most of their prime location on the front. Some houses have been converted to shops, others have gone up a storey, or had new bay windows installed. I think most people are better off and maybe they're happier now. I just don't know.

The Sloop Inn and 'fly away' chimneys, St Ives, 1912. This is one of my most prized photographs because it
some interesting features, and tells me about the lives of ordinary people long ago. There is also the famous Sl
Inn on the harbour. There were several ancient pubs in the harbour where sailors could have a drink, but r
only the Sloop, a building of great antiquity, survives. The others, like the Globe, the White Hart and the S
Aground, have closed and are now used as shops. Those chimneys fascinate me, especially the ones leaning i
the wind and defying gravity. They seem likely to 'fly away' at any moment. The little boy in the foregroun
watching the gang approach, and I wonder what he's thinking. The lady with the splendid pram takes cer
stage. I wonder why all those ladies are hanging around outside the pub with their hats and aprons? Not drink
surely; perhaps they are waiting for the fishing boats and the task of handling, gutting or salting down the ca
Today the lads sit outside the Sloop in the sun, with beer bellies and bare chests, and watch the world go
Maybe I'll join them next year in the new millennium – an old 'drop-out' with whiskers, a hat and a small beer

St Eia Street, St Ives, *c.* 1939. This is how the town looked before the tourists came: a quiet little street in Downlong, with Burrow Road at the top and Wheel Dream at the bottom. Teetotal Street runs parallel with this one on the right and Back Street East likewise on the left. Most of these houses are back-to-back. The house in the foreground, with the steps, had one door in St Eia Street and another door in Teetotal Street; also, one room went over the room of a house in Teetotal Street. This arrangement is known as a 'flying freehold' and was not uncommon. In those days Couches shop was at the Burrow Road end and it seemed to sell everything. Most back streets had a corner shop, but now they have all gone. You can see the gas lighting and the washing lines in the street. Halfway up on the left is Mr Bennett's. Nicknamed 'Doctor Us', he was a retired fisherman who had a gold earring in his ear, and always wore a peaked cap, Guernsey sweater and smock. Today most of these houses have been modernised and are summer lets or second homes.

Washday, St Ives, 1926. This was a typical scene in Downlong on washday, with washing hanging out to dry over the street. Years ago St Ives was divided into two halves known as Uplong and Downlong, with the Market House being the division between them. Downlong was the home of the fishing community, while the sea captains and professional classes lived in Uplong. Much of Downlong is built between the harbour and Porthmeor, which was originally a sandbank. Now there is a maze of little streets, passages and courtyards with interesting names like Teetotal Street, The Digey, Bethesda Place and St Eia Street.

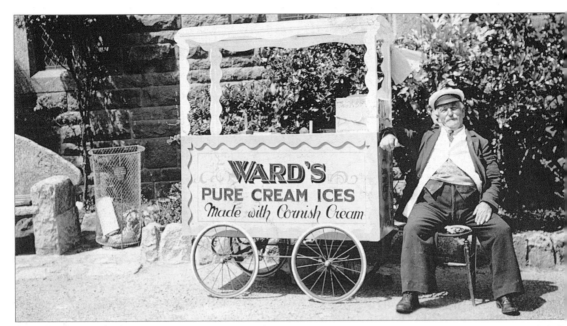

Cap'n William Henry Bosanquet selling Ward's icecream outside the Catholic Church, St Ives, *c*. 1935. It charming photograph of a St Ives man going about his business. William Henry confidently sits for the camera v his beautiful icecream cart complete with massive cone, biscuits, wrapping paper and spoked wheels. He was bor St Ives in 1863 and first went to sea in local sailing coasters at the age of fourteen. At fifteen he went on his first c water voyage as a cabin boy on a square rigger, crossing the line and rounding two Capes, and returned home a sixteen. He said he went as a boy and returned a man. He joined the Hain Shipping Line and sailed with them boatswain (bos'n) for many years before he retired from the sea in the early 1920s. William Henry had tried a jobs ashore, like mining in Wheal Trenwith, but the lure of the sea always pulled him back. Later on, he ran beach at Portscatho with his wife for a few summers, then turned his hand to selling icecream for Mr Ward. He always called Cap'n as a mark of respect by his fellow seafarers. Towards the end of his life he became bedridden didn't lack visitors, and he would regale them with tales of his life at sea. He died in November 1949, aged eighty after a long adventurous life.

ant Mine, 1900. Dramatically situated on the cliff edge, near Geevor Mine and Pendeen, Levant is famous for
ong working life and its undersea riches of tin and copper. Its life really spanned from about the end of the
teenth century to 1930, and there was a mile of workings extending beneath the Atlantic. Copper and tin
s are in a vertical plane and you must always dig deeper to extract the ore. In 1919, when the mine was 350
oms deep, a primitive lifting beam, called a man-engine, collapsed. Thirty-one miners were killed. Despite this
ster the mine continued working until the economic situation forced it to close in 1930. The Geevor Mine
rated part of the Levant workings later but now all work has ceased. The small white house on the right is the
ne house, which still contains its winding engine (the Cornish term is 'whim') in a working condition. Its task
to raise ore from deep levels via Skip Shaft, seen with its headgear just behind the house. The winding engine
saved from destruction by an enthusiast who bought it for £25. The Trevithick Society was formed to save
machines, and now the engine house and its beam whim are in the hands of the National Trust and open to
public. Behind this engine house is a taller, more impressive but ruined engine house which once contained a
m engine to pump water from Engine Shaft, marked by the taller headgear on the right. The whole area
ınd Pendeen and St Just is filled with reminders of Cornwall's mining heritage.

ɔosite) Market Square, St Just-in-Penwith, c. 1912. The most westerly town in England, this was the centre of a
y mining area in the last century. Mines like Geevor, Levant and Botallack were perched on the cliffside,
lucing large quantities of tin and copper. St Just Church was built in about 1486 and restored in 1865. Note
ne old tower and pinnacles. Inside are two fifteenth-century wall paintings, one depicting St George and the
gon and the other Christ of the Trades. The Wellington Hotel is still busy, and in Bank Square across the road
the grassy banks of the Plain-an-Gwarry enclosure where mystery plays were staged years ago. Further on
n this road you reach impressive Cape Cornwall and the dreaded Brisons rocks.

Sennen Cove and Whitesand Bay, *c.* 1918. This is a good view of the bay and the road to Sennen village winding up the hill. Sennen doesn't seem to change very much. There are two parts: the Village on top of the cliff, which is the most westerly village in mainland Britain, and Sennen Cove, the old fishing village seen here. Whitesand Bay with its magnificent beach also sweeps away in the distance. The breakwater on the left is designed to allow the Sennen Cove lifeboat to put to sea in heavy weather. The lifeboat station was established in Sennen in 1853 because of its proximity to the dangerous reefs off Lands End.

Sennen post office, Lands End, 1913. This is a charming photograph of ancient thatched cottages and a lovely old car, registration number AF 348. The lady stands smiling in the doorway, with her child in her arms, while the driver waits nonchalantly by his car. The post office here was combined with a shop. There is an enamelled sign advertising Liptons Tea and what looks like a £1000 reward poster! This also looks like the road that leads down to Lands End with scattered houses and farms in the distance.

Happy Lands End visitors, 1958. Well, we've just about come to the end of my book and I thought I'd show you a happy group of visitors to Lands End. I don't know who they are or where they came from, but I don't think it matters. They came in 1958 and saw a little of Cornwall and had a good time. Even Americans would need more than a day to see Cornwall! We have so much to offer and I believe our future lies in decentralised government and tourism, even if the Celts and Saxons have to work together towards common goals.

Lands End and Longships Lighthouse, *c.* 1930. This is the most westerly point in Britain. The Longships Lighthouse is less than 2 miles offshore, and about 8 miles to the south is the Wolf Rock Lighthouse. The Scilly Isles are 28 miles distant, and in between lies the fabled land of Lyonesse which sank beneath the waves, destroyed by a freak tidal wave. Then there is America, thousands of miles across the Atlantic Ocean. Ships keep coming and going. It's a place of many fond welcomes and many sad goodbyes.

ACKNOWLEDGEMENTS

I am extremely grateful to all the following for the loan of photographs and postcards: Mr R. Down, Dr G. Hones, Mr and Mrs P. Manning (Torpoint Archives), Mr D. Nancollas (Saltash Heritage), Mr C. Nute, Mrs L. Smith, Mr and Mrs B. Stevens and Mr W. Young.

Also I must thank the following: Sir Richard Carew Pole for permission to include the portrait of Sir John Carew Pole; Dr Charles Causley for permission to include his photograph; Mr D. Pengelly for permission to show my photograph of Mr and Mrs A.J. Pengelly; and the staff at the Cornwall Family History Society, Truro, who helped me to unravel the Argalls' family tree.

I am particularly indebted to the following for their original work: Mr A. Kitteridge, author of *Passenger Steamers of the River Tamar*; Mr R. Lacey, for his many articles on Cornish photographers; Mr M. Tangye, for his book *Tehidy and the Bassets*; Mr R. Burt, for his book *Cornish Mining*; Mr L.F. Barham, for his publication *Cornwall's Electric Tramcars*; and Mr P.Q. Treloar, for his Sutton publication *Around Helston and the Lizard*.

I have only detailed the work of five Cornish photographers in this publication, but the other postcards herein were produced by famous publishers like Frith and Valentine, as well as by less well-known publishers and a few that remain anonymous. I thank them all for providing a pictorial record of Cornish life in the twentieth century.

Lastly I thank my dear wife Pam, for her support during the preparation of this book.